Praise for the Book

"Joseph Bruchac is among our wisest and most enduring storytellers. His voice, his flute, and his tales are grace notes. *A Year of Moons* speaks to the cyclic nature of Western Abenaki home ground. Within these pages, readers will find an incantation of attention, patience, and what endures through the generations: a fierce love of place."

—Terry Tempest Williams,
Author of *The Hour of Land*

"Bruchac's *A Year of Moons* weaves seasonal observations, remembrances, and stories into each chapter, engaging the reader's imagination, heart, and senses, and then wraps up each one with beautiful haiku. A journey not to be missed!"

—Traci Sorell,
Author of *Powwow Day*

A YEAR OF MOONS

STORIES FROM THE ADIRONDACK FOOTHILLS

BY
JOSEPH BRUCHAC

Fulcrum Publishing
Wheat Ridge, Colorado

Library of Congress Cataloging-in-Publication Data

Names: Bruchac, Joseph, 1942- author.
Title: A year of moons : stories from the Adirondack foothills / by Joseph Bruchac.
Description: Wheat Ridge, Colorado : Fulcrum Publishing, [2022]
Identifiers: LCCN 2021059403 | ISBN 9781682753224 (paperback)
Subjects: LCSH: Abenaki Indians--New York (State)--Adirondack
  Mountains--Social life and customs. | Traditional ecological
  knowledge--New York (State)--Adirondack Mountains.
Classification: LCC E99.A13 B793 2022 | DDC 974.004/9734--dc23/
eng/20220103
LC record available at https://lccn.loc.gov/2021059403

Printed in the United States
0 9 8 7 6 5 4 3 2 1

Fulcrum Publishing
3970 Youngfield Street
Wheat Ridge, Colorado 80033
(800) 992-2908 • (303) 277-1623
www.fulcrumbooks.com

CONTENTS

INTRODUCTION: A YEAR OF MOONS / 9

    On Haiku / 12

ABENAKI MOONS / 15

by Jesse Bowman Bruchac and Joseph Elie Joubert

ALAMIKOS: NEW YEAR'S GREETING MOON / 18

    Anhaldam Mawi / 18

    Black Squirrel / 22

MOZOKAS: MOOSE MOON / 28

    Moose Hunting Moon / 28

SOGALIKAS: MOON OF FLOWING / 34

    Maple Sugar Moon / 34

    Falling / 43

CEGWALIKA: FROG MOON / 49

I Brake for Toads / 49

Tadpoles / 56

KIKAS: MOON OF PLANTING / 65

Butterflies / 65

Mountain Lions / 67

Spring Rain / 76

NOKKAHIGAS: MOON OF HOEING / 80

Ko-Ko-Leeyo-Kway! / 80

Smiling Joe / 85

Gray Foxes / 92

MSKIKOIKAS: MOON OF STRAWBERRIES / 98

Strawberries / 98

Dreams / 106

Libraries / 113

The Blanket Tree / 118

PAD8GIKAS: MOON OF THUNDER / 130

Squirrels / 130

Bamboo Flute / 136

Six Degrees / 141

KAWAKWENIKAS: GATHERER (WILD HARVEST) MOON / 150

An August Morning / 150

Guilt / 156

Harvest Moon / 159

SKAMONKAS: CORN MOON / 165

Deer / 165

Walking / 170

PENIBAGOS: MOON OF LEAVES FALLING / 173

Falling Leaves Moon / 173

Bears / 176

Fear / 186

Moose Spirits / 191

MZATONOS: MOON OF FREEZING / 197

Thin Ice / 197

New Snow / 204

PEBONKAS: MOON OF LONG NIGHTS / 208

Fire Making / 208

Breathe / 216

ABOUT THE AUTHOR / 223

INTRODUCTION

A YEAR OF MOONS

One of the things that the Native people of this continent found curious about Europeans was their concept of something they called "time." To some of us, it seemed as if these white people worshipped it—in the form of the clocks and watches that appeared to rule their days. That was especially obvious, for example, in the way the Catholic missionaries had to pray at certain "times of the day"—as opposed to praying and giving thanks constantly, which was more the Indigenous way of doing things.

My own Native ancestors had to make up a new word for those tick-tocking devices to which our new neighbors were constantly paying so much attention. So, the word for clock in Abenaki became *pa-pee-zo-kwazik*—"the thing that makes much noise but does nothing useful."

It just didn't make much sense back then. Nor, to some of us, still today.

Take, for example, the even more abstract concept of what is called "daylight saving time," when those clocks would be moved an hour ahead, and then an hour back, depending on what part of the year it was. It made as much sense as cutting off the end of a piece of rope and tying it onto the other end. Then, after half of the year had passed untying it and fastening it back to the end where it originally had been connected.

It doesn't mean that we lacked a way of telling time. Among all of our more than 500 tribal nations in what is now called the United States there was an awareness of the yearly cycle, the circle of changing seasons repeated year after year. We closely observed the daily coming and going of light through Kisos, the Great Sun, and the nightly appearance and the movement of the lights in the sky—Nanibonsad, the Night Traveler Moon, and the Awatawesuk, the Little Distant Ones, the stars.

Among most of our Tribal Nations, the most common way of marking the course of a year was through the moon. Its waxing and waning in the night sky was visible to everyone, and it was a clearly experienced, regular period of time from one full moon to the next—twenty-eight days, with a total of thirteen full moons making up one year.

It was also obvious, from close observation of the natural world, that different things happened during different moons. That varied from place to place because of the differences in climate, as well as all the other aspects of the ecosystem. So, each of those moons had a descriptive name—though the names would be different from one part of the continent to the next. The salmon were never running on the Great Plains, and there were no buffalo calves shedding their winter fur on the Pacific Coast. Those moon names reminded people of what they should be doing or be aware of, as well as to be thankful for the gifts that part of the great cycle of seasons was bringing them yet again.

So it was through the names of the moons that I decided to structure this book that blends my memories, experiences, and observations of nature through the course of a year, mostly within this part of our Western Abenaki homelands. It is the ecosystem that maps now designate as the Adirondack region of present-day Upstate New York, a place I've lived my whole life and never intend to leave. I expect my ashes to be mixed into its glacial soil.

For more than thirty years I've had a now-yellowed typed piece of paper stuck to the wall above my desk with those names of the moons written in English and in Abenaki as they were given to me by Attian Lolo/Stephen Laurent, a beloved friend and Abenaki elder. Those are the names I have used here.

Most of them are pretty obvious, such as Moon of Strawberries or Falling Leaves Moon. But, the first one may need some explaining—the New Year's Greeting Moon. It corresponds to early January, marking the beginning of a new year in the middle of winter, a time when we should think of new beginnings. Our Old People knew that to correctly start a new year, we needed to let go of things from the past year that might hold us back, especially grudges, guilt, and anger. So the practice was created of going from lodge to lodge saying, "*Anhaldam mawi kassipalilawalan:* Forgive me for any wrong I may have done you."

I hope, as you read these stories, take this journey with me through the moons, that what I share may awaken in you a deeper awareness of those ancient cycles still going on all around us in the natural world. It is the realest of worlds, the one we all need to remember and treat with respect.

ON HAIKU

For several years now it has been my practice to write a haiku every morning—usually while walking my dog through the woods along the old roads here in the foothills of the Kaydeross Range at the southern edge of the Adirondack Park.

The poems included in this book are gleaned from the 375 I wrote over the span of one calendar year.

I first began studying haiku while in college, six decades ago. My constant companions since 1961 have been the Blyth anthologies, which include not just the translations of haiku poems by the great masters—especially Matsuo Bashō, Yosa Buson, and Kobayashi Issa—but also the original versions of the poems in Japanese and commentaries on each.

So, I have long been aware that a haiku poem is more than just syllabics—three lines of five, seven, and five syllables. Even the old Japanese poets often padded their lines to reach seventeen syllables by inserting words that had no real meaning other than to add syllables—such as *kana*.

Many contemporary writers of haiku in the English-speaking world ignore that five/seven/five syllable count and have produced some very good and memorable modern haiku.

What makes a poem a haiku? Here are several of the characteristics that I believe constitute a haiku:

It is brief — no more than two or three lines.

It evokes a season.

It does not use simile or metaphor.

It is steeped in the observation or experience of the natural world.

Also, one of my haiku teachers, Tai-yul Kim, said to me that one of the most central elements of a true haiku is that it produces a sensation of "ah-ness."

Although some teachers, especially those working with grade school students, describe haiku as simple and easy to do, Tai-yul Kim's opinion was quite different. He described the writing we did in his class as "attempts at haiku."

In writing my own haiku, I have chosen to follow the five/seven/five line count of what might be called English haiku. I don't think it's necessary, but I like the form—just as I like the form and the seventeen lines of a sonnet.

Also, though we haven't included any in this book of essays, I often include a photograph taken at the time the poem was written when I post it—as I sometimes do—on Facebook and Twitter. I feel that, in doing this, I am tiptoe-ing in the tradition of those Japanese haiku masters, many of whom were fine artists and included their paintings with their poems.

ABENAKI MOONS

BY JESSE BOWMAN BRUCHAC AND
JOSEPH ELIE JOUBERT

The year is commenced from the new moon preceding Christmas. Months are counted by new moons, and the first day of each new moon is the first day of the month. There is also a name for each full moon.

Each new moon is fourteen days (two weeks), and each full moon is fourteen days with twenty-eight days in each complete cycle of the moon. As in some years there are thirteen moons (twenty-six counting new and full moons), then the Abenakis skip the new and full moons between July and August, and they call this Abonamwikizos (Let This Moon Go). It is used like the modern leap year to keep the calendar on track.

In the following you will notice that there are, in some cases, several names for the same moons. All are acceptable in the language, and it's usually up to the speaker to decide which is to be used. However, some are used dependent on setting or region. In addition, as described earlier, moons do not all cover the same periods of time. Some are shorter than a month, while others are longer; some are names specifically for the full moon during a given month, and still others are names of specific celebrations during a moon.

Also included are literal translations with additional meanings in parentheses. Some have several possible translations, all of which could be correct, as Western Abenaki names often have more than one meaning. Further, there may be more than one Abenaki name used for many of these moons, each name reflecting something that is happening in the natural world at that time.

ala: and, or

8: pronounced like the "un" sound in skunk

Alamikos ala Anhaldamawikizos—Greetings Maker or Forgiveness Moon: January

Pia8dagos—Falling in Pieces or Branches Maker: February

Sigwankas ala Sigwanikizosak—Spring Maker (Birds Return Maker, Melt Maker) or Spring Moons: March, April, and May

Mozokas—Moose Maker (Hunter): March

Sogalikas ala Sogalikizos ala 8maswikizos—Sugar Maker

or Sugar Moon or When We Catch Fish: March, April
(April was formerly called **Mekwaskwikizos** [the Great
Cold Moon], but since the Abenaki were deprived of
their rich settlements on the Kennebec, it has been
changed.)

Kikas ala Kikaikizos—Field Maker or Moon in Which We
Plant (the Planter): May

Nokkahigas ala Mskikoikas—the Hoer or Strawberry Moon
(Full Strawberry Moon): June

Temaskikos ala Sataikas ala Pad8gikas—Hay Cutter or
Blueberry Maker or Thunder Moon: July

Mijow8gankas ala Michinikizosak—Meal Maker or Eating
Moons: August and September

Temez8was ala Kawakwenikas—Harvester (Cutter) or
Gatherer (Wild Harvester): August

Skamonkas—Corn Maker: September

Penibagos—Leaf Fall Maker: October

Mezatanos ala Mezatanokas—Freezing Current (River)
One or Freezing Current Maker: November

Pebonkas ala Kchikizos—Winter Maker or Great Moon:
December

ALAMIKOS

NEW YEAR'S GREETING MOON

ANHALDAM MAWI

There's a fresh coating of snow on the ground outside our cabin as I look to see who's coming to the fourteen feeders we keep filled with black oil sunflower seeds year-round.

It's January here in our Adirondack foothills. The time of Alamikos, the Abenaki term for the first moon of the new year. In English, it's the New Year's Greeting Moon,. It's the time when people would go from one wigwam to another—nowadays one house to another—and speak the New Year's greeting.

Anhaldam mawi kassipalilawalan.

Its meaning, translated into English, is "Forgive me for any wrong I may have done you."

It's a simple thing to say, but its meaning is so deep. It's a recognition of the fact that there is always more than one way to look at any situation, any human interaction, because it would be said not just to people you know you've wronged, but to everyone. Everyone.

Think of the times when your own feelings were injured by a word or deed from someone who was totally oblivious to the fact that they'd wounded you. It happens more often than we may realize. We're in a hurry and we brush someone off. We make a remark offhandedly or say something that we may think is humorous but in fact cuts another person to the quick.

I'm too busy to talk just now.

I like it that you never worry about how you look.

That was stupid.

You're not that fat.

Where'd you get that shirt? From Good Will?

What butcher cuts your hair?

Or the remark made from the audience to bluesman Guy Davis this past Saturday evening as he performed at Saratoga Springs's famous folk club the Caffe Lena: "Do you have songs for anybody under the age of twenty?"—the comment admittedly made by a fourteen-year-old. This prompted Guy to say as we were talking while he was packing up that it was karmic payback for something he said when he was that age.

He was at a theater with his mother, actress and civil rights activist Ruby Dee, and he said in response to a famous actress when she asked him his opinion of tragedy: "Tragedy bores me."

Forgive me for any wrong I may have done you, even if I didn't intend to do it. Or if I did.

Think about it. Think of what it means to start a year this way. What it means to make that sincere attempt to make amends. And to be assured that others in your community, through that simple statement, that caring visit, want to begin anew.

Forgive me for any wrong I may have done.

It reminds me of something I first heard more than four decades ago while I was a volunteer teacher in Keta, Ghana, a West African town located on a long sand peninsula (Keta means "the head of the sand" in the Ewe language) between a giant lagoon and the Gulf of Guinea.

Each morning, with the exception of the one day sacred to the sea god, the wind from the ocean would bring me the sound of the fishermen chanting as they pulled their long nets in to shore. When I was not teaching one of the six classes on my daily schedule, I would often go down to the beach and help them pull, a welcome helping hand that they'd often repay by giving me a few fish from the catch.

As we pulled, our feet churning the sand together, the men around me would be singing songs in Ewe, all of us kept in sync by the song and the beat of a double-throated iron bell.

And those songs, ah, those songs. Each one of them was nothing less than a musical proverb. And I will never forget the meaning of one of those songs in particular.

Here's how Nelson Amegashie, one of my Third Form students, and I translated it into English:

> *No person knows who all their enemies are.*
> *The very way a man walks may offend someone.*
> *Only God knows who all your enemies are.*
> *Therefore always try to do what is right.*
> *No one but God knows all your enemies.*

It's another reminder, one I've carried with me ever since then. A reminder to attempt to be mindful of what I do and what I say. But also a reminder that, being a mere human in the company of other equally fallible folks, the possibility will always exist of upsetting another by my very existence.

So what better way to start the year than this? This greeting—as fresh as that new snow covering the brown grass of the lawn—I send out now to all my friends—as well as any who may think themselves my enemies.

Anhaldam mawi kassipalilawalan.

Chickadees dart in
one by one to the feeder
each takes one black seed

This snow-covered pond
tracks telling countless stories
of those who crossed it

BLACK SQUIRREL

This late January, there's one in the woods just beyond my back-yard here in Porter Corners. It seems to be shyer than its gray brothers and sisters. Hasn't yet bellied up to the bar with the other squirrels that come to our feeders every day. I've watched it as it hops nervously across the snow, stopping every now and then to sit up, its paws held up in front of it like an elderly person clutching a purse. But, though I've clicked a few pics of it from fifty feet away, it has yet to get any closer to the house.

Melanism. Black fur. A fairly common color phase in gray squirrels, especially in certain areas. Such as in parts of western New York. If you visit Niagara Falls and check out the trees in the park areas above the river there's a good chance you'll see more than one black squirrel—as I did the last time I was there two years ago. Squirrels can live a dozen or more years in the wild, as many as twenty-five in captivity. So there's a good chance some of those black squirrels I saw will still be there.

But black squirrels tend to be rare here in the North Country.

I've always been fascinated by them. As was my dad who was a taxidermist. Joseph Bruchac, the Adirondack taxidermist. Bearing the same name as his father. And a bunch of Slovak Bruchacs before him. I still have people confuse me with my father. Despite the fact that he passed away more than three decades ago, every now and then I get a phone call from someone wanting to know if I still tan skins or if I can mount a deer head for them.

I used to hunt gray squirrels. Not for fun, but because they make good eating, especially their muscular hind quarters. Squirrel stew is an old favorite in American Indian diets. As a matter of fact, that came up when I was interviewing the grandson of Native American Olympian Jim Thorpe for a documentary film my friend Tom Weidlinger and I did called *Jim Thorpe, the World's Greatest Athlete*.

"Jim's favorite dish," his grandson said, "was squirrel with biscuits and gravy."

So it was that when I was a grad student at Syracuse University back in the mid-sixties, with not much income between me and my wife, Carol, we supplemented our diet with wild game—pheasant, partridge, and gray squirrel—that I hunted only a couple of miles beyond married student housing. There was a forest of oak woods there back then (a forest that sadly has been replaced by a quarry, a four-lane highway, and several housing developments).

Squirrels and oak forests go together. That's not just because squirrels like to eat those acorns, but because the gray squirrel is one of the main vectors for spreading and maintaining oak forests. The squirrel's habit of burying its stores combined with forgetting where all of them are results in the growth of new trees. A simple formula. Obsessive-compulsive behavior + long-term memory loss = reforestation. The first person to really notice this relationship between squirrels and forests and write about it was none other than Henry David Thoreau, who once said, "The squirrel that you kill in jest dies in earnest." In his essay, "The Dispersion of Seeds," published in 1862 long after his death, he praises the squirrels, those "planters of the forest."

One day, back in 1965, when I was talking with my father over the phone, he asked if I had ever seen any black squirrels out there because he'd heard that there were some in the Syracuse area.

"As a matter of fact," I said, "I saw one the other day, but it was too skittish to get close to it."

"If you can manage to get it for me," Dad replied, "I'd really like to have it to mount."

Pause here for one of my father's favorite taxidermy jokes. (Alas, he had many of them.)

A man comes into a taxidermist's shop with a pair of squirrels.

"You want these mounted?" the taxidermist asks.

"No, I'd just like them shaking hands."

A couple of days later, I made the short trek back to the place where I'd caught a glimpse of that black squirrel. I had my grandfather's old 12 gauge shotgun loaded with size 4 birdshot. The terrain was rough where I'd seen it, an area with large boulders and lots of brush, and just as hilly as one would expect, it being part of the traditional lands of the Onondaga nation of the Haudenosaunee. Onondaga means the People of the Hills.

I took my time as I picked my way through that landscape, looking down as often as I looked up. My shotgun was cradled under my right arm, a shell in the chamber, but the safety on. I'd come to an old fence and had been careful to put the gun down before crossing it, only reaching back to bring the gun through after I was on the other side. I remembered the lesson of my great-uncle Harry Dunham. As a young man he'd accidentally shot himself across the belly with a shotgun when he was trying to crawl through a fence. He'd survived, but the scar tissue there pulled so tight that he never could stand fully upright for the rest of his life. Bent over like a comma.

Then I caught a glimpse of something dark near the top of a distant oak. It was that black squirrel. I began to stalk closer, keeping as many trees as possible between us and pressing off the safety. And perhaps because I had my eyes on that squirrel, I wasn't watching the ground as carefully as I could have. Or maybe it would have made no difference—because the mat of leaves and fallen small limbs that had bridged a hidden gap between buried boulders was so tight that they perfectly resembled level ground in front of me. Until I stepped there and that far-from-solid surface gave way beneath me like the Burmese Tiger Pit built by Rainsford in the story "The Most Dangerous Game."

From that point on, everything slowed down. It was as if I'd been detached from my body and was watching it all from above. The shower of sticks and dead leaves scattering around me. The loaded shotgun knocked from my hand, turning in midair. Its stock hitting the ground. The tongue of flame erupting from its barrel as it discharged. And me, still in midair, my eyes on that gun, twisting my body so that the load of lead barely missed me.

And then I landed. Not on sharpened stakes, as this was no human-made trap but rather one fashioned by coincidence. A thick bed of fallen leaves and twigs cushioned my fall. However, it was hard enough to knock the wind out of me. I stayed there for a while, regaining my breath as I looked up at the beautiful slant of blue sky visible above me. My left hand was on my chest, my right hand rested on the warm barrel of my grandfather's gun.

And when my breath returned, I just spoke two words. Not to any person, but to everything around me. Including that black squirrel I was definitely not going to keep hunting.

Thank you, I said. I sat up then, unloaded the gun and carefully placed the shells into my vest pocket. More than fifty years have passed since then. I still clean my grandfather's shotgun regularly, keep it safely stowed away—with the shells locked in a desk drawer—but I've never tried to shoot another squirrel.

This cold morning I've counted five different gray squirrels out my window, as well as one red squirrel who seems to think she has a long-term lease on the larger feeder. It's not surprising that there are so many now. Between December and February is one of the two breeding seasons for grays. (Not just a time for shaking hands.) And, as I watch, the large black one arrives, coming headfirst down the trunk of the biggest pine. Maybe one of those nests that will soon be filled with hairless little ones will yield a black juvenile or two when they venture out on their own in May or June.

And perhaps, in the years to come, it may not be that unusual around here to see a black squirrel.

Feet almost frozen
ice crunches underfoot
five more miles to go

MOZOKAS

MOOSE MOON

MOOSE HUNTING
MOON

On the desk next to my computer is a Plaster of Paris cast of a print my son Jim took a week ago from the marshy ground above Little Bucket Pond, two miles from my cabin. Bigger than my outspread hand, it's a hoof print. Not that of a deer, but a moose.

Fifty years ago, a print like that would've been unheard of in our parts. Back then, moose were gone from New York State, aside from a single animal now and then wandering far from its usual range in Maine—in most cases suffering from a brain worm contracted from the feces of the white-tailed deer.

When I was in my twenties studying wildlife conservation at Cornell University we were told that the moose—shot off more than a century ago—would never return to our region. It was because of a parasitic larva of a meningeal worm with a name longer than some sentences—*Parelaphostrongylus tenuis*, or brain worm, as it is commonly known. Although brain worm seldom causes death in its primary carrier, the white-tailed deer, exposure to the feces of the white tail can infect the moose. Once inside the body of a moose, there's no cure. The larvae travel to the spinal cord and the brain, causing severe neurological damage that results in the moose becoming disoriented, walking in aimless circles, eventually dying.

Those giant ungulates were gone, never to return—like the mountain lion, the wolf, and the elk. That's what I was taught in college.

What I heard from Native elders was a different story. Sometimes it was explained to me through traditional tales, sometimes pointed out to me in the natural world where things don't exist in neat, straight lines but rather in cycles. There, in the natural world—as with the seasons, for example—things pass and then return. The overall message, from those stories and what I was taught to observe, was a pretty simple one. Rather than us humans having to fix things (that we broke), the best we can do is to stop doing whatever it is that mucks it all up. Then step back and leave it alone. Allow it to come back on its own.

That is what the moose have done here in the Adirondacks. It has been a gradual thing, that return to their original range. They spread from Maine, where healthy herds had survived, into nearby New Hampshire. As fewer lands were clear-cut for timber or stripped of trees to make fields, the northern forest spread. And so did the beings who knew it as home. Before long, moose were common again in Vermont, and by the 1980s, they appeared in the Adirondacks.

Today, in 2022, the moose population in New York State—especially the Adirondacks—continues to grow. As in New Hampshire and Vermont, especially where deer herds are abundant, brain worm has been found here, but it hasn't stopped the increase, and it appears that moose populations are stable and will keep growing. A 2019 helicopter survey spotted more than eighty-three groups of moose here in northernmost New York State. The estimate is that there are more than 400 of them here now.

Moose were important to my ancestors. We carefully used their meat, their bones, their skin. The time of hunting them was this part of the winter, when a man on snowshoes could both track and catch up to them in the deep drifts. That's why this time of year was called Moose Moon, Mozokas, when you went out to bring back the moose you'd chosen to harvest.

Hunting was not a chance thing among our Old People. Because hunters back then understood the animals in their territory so well, they knew where they were at any given time. They could pick the individual animal that was the correct one to take when the time was right.

A group of Athabascan hunters in Alaska (where the traditions of moose hunting are still much like our own were years ago) said to a disbelieving ethnologist, "Today we are going to go out to shoot a three-year-old bull moose at noon at the junction of three streams." To that white man's surprise, that is exactly what they did.

But, it's more than just knowing the habits of an animal. More than recognizing which one would be the right one to harvest without harming the integrity of the herd. There is an ancient connection between humans and the animals that we hunt. It's especially visible in our stories of taking a moose.

The Cree are our Algonquin cousins to the north, and there is a Cree story that reflects the Abenaki understanding of that hunter-to-hunted relationship.

A group of moose were sitting in their Winter Lodge around the fire. Suddenly a pipe came floating in through the lodge door.

"Do not take that pipe," one of the old moose said.

But a younger full-grown moose reached out and took it.

As soon as he did so, that moose found himself running through deep snow, human hunters following him on snowshoes. He could not escape, and they shot him with their arrows.

Then, before they did anything else, they offered him a gift of tobacco.

"Thank you," the hunters said. "May you continue to run."

The next thing that happened was that the young moose woke up. He was back in the lodge, alive again and holding the pipe and that tobacco.

"You see," he said, "it is all right. Those humans gave me a gift and showed me the right kind of respect. As long as they do that, it is all right that we offer them our bodies."

A Penobscot friend of ours in Maine just posted on Facebook a picture he took of the moose that allowed him to harvest it. He is sitting next to it, its huge body dwarfing his. In his hand is the tobacco he offered that moose.

I'm sure he spoke in Penobscot those words that are almost the same in Abenaki. We say them still to any being that has allowed us the gift of its body, for we know that its spirit watches to make sure we remember thanks and respect.

May you continue to run.

New tracks in the snow
show me two moose passed this way
just before the dawn

Doe raises her head
looks straight at me through the brush
standing still, I smile

Snowbanks retreating
five crows hop along the ground
pick at the new earth

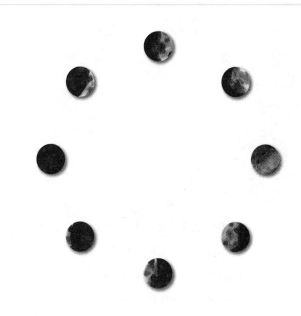

SOGALIKAS

MOON OF FLOWING

MAPLE SUGAR MOON

March in the Adirondack foothills. A feel in the air of things starting to stir. Days growing longer. The first light through the windows of my cabin on the southeast flank of Glass Factory Mountain waking me earlier each day.

I step outside, bare feet melting the gray frost on the deck. Spread my arms and breathe deep as I go through a series of tai chi moves. And though the land is still caught in the winter chill—10 degrees Fahrenheit this morning—it's as if the cold cannot cut as deep now. By noon it will be 40 degrees.

It's time to tap the maple trees.

Sogalikas. The Moon of Making Maple Syrup. Or, translated more literally from the Abenaki language, the Flowing Moon. For it is now Sigwaniwi, the melting away time: when the moisture of earth is drawn up by trees as they awaken to the lengthening of the days, snow melting from the warmth of the sun.

There are traditional tales of how making sweet syrup from the trees came to be. The simplest is that a squirrel chewed into the trunk of a maple. Someone, most likely from one of our northeastern Algonquin nations, had left a basket by the base of that tree and the flowing sap filled up that basket. Not a woven basket, of course. One that was made as we still make watertight baskets today by folding pliable bark— most likely birch—into a basket shape and pegging or sewing it together.

When that person tasted the water in her basket, she found that it was sweet. And then when that water was used for cooking, it was sweeter still.

The first white man to comment on making maple syrup was John Smith in the seventeenth century. He wrote in his journals about how the Powhatan women collected the sap from the trees by making a V-shaped gouge with an axe and putting a bark basket beneath it. After which they poured the sap into wooden troughs. Each morning they would take the ice off the top of the trough and throw it away. They assured him that the sugar did not freeze, and, indeed, Smith noted, the sap got sweeter each time they skimmed off the ice. After doing this several times they'd then boil the rest down to maple syrup.

It does take a lot of sap to make syrup. The rule of thumb is about forty to one—forty quarts of sap for one of syrup. One way it was done before metal evaporators was to put the syrup into a dugout canoe and then drop in red-hot rocks.

I remember the first time I tasted maple sap. I was with my grandparents and only five years old. We'd pulled up to the Ferrys' house. Three elderly cousins of my grandmother's. A brother and two sisters together, none of them ever married, all of them in their eighties. Ethel, Edna, and Pearly.

Edna was the one who came clomping up to the car. She was wearing knee boots, one of their late father's old red wool coats, a scarf wrapped around her head. Her cheeks were as red from the cold as that scarlet scarf. She had a gray metal bucket in her hands. She'd just unhooked it from the maple closest to the road.

My window was rolled down and she leaned through it.

"Have a taste," she said, "it's sweet as a spring day."

I shrank back in my seat with my hands over my mouth. I was shy back then and a little afraid of anything new. Especially Edna decked out in those crimson colors.

Thus my first taste of maple sap straight from the tree was delayed. Though not that long. After we'd all gone inside the big old house, I waited for my chance. And while everyone was talking, I slipped out the back door to another tree where I'd spied a bucket hanging from one of those hooks I later learned to call a spile. I cautiously unhooked it. There was only an inch or so of sap in the bucket and it wasn't too heavy for me. I looked around to make sure I wasn't being watched, then lifted it up and drank. I mostly soaked the front of my shirt, but for that cold, wet, and sticky taste, it was worth it. It was as sweet—in a subtle way—as the breath of a spring day. I hung the bucket back up. No one noticed me slipping back in, even though the back door did slip out of my wet hands and slam.

All five of those old people were looking at the ceiling as I crept back into the room, my grandfather stifling a cough that sounded a little like a laugh. Nor was my soggy condition mentioned all the way home. Though my grandmother did remark—as soon as we got out of the old blue Plymouth— that I might want to change my clothes.

"Seeing as how, Sonny, you seem to have got some snow on you—in some inadvertent way."

Which remark set my grandfather to coughing again.

I imagine that by now the sap house behind the Onondaga Nation School (ONS) has been made ready for this year's flow. ONS is one of my favorite schools, right smack in the middle of the Onondaga Reservation that is itself the heart of the Iroquois Confederacy. (I'd say that Onondaga is right next to Syracuse, New York—except the opposite is true. Onondaga, that place among the hills, was here centuries before any Greek name was grafted onto the land. Further, a good part of the city of Syracuse is on land still owned by the Onondaga Nation and leased to the city.)

I remember the first time I visited the ONS sap house where Native students, from kindergarten on up, take part in that old ceremony of gathering and boiling down that renews the bond between the people and the maple—the Leader, the Chief of the Trees, as it is called. It's at this time of year when the Haudenosaunee people give Thanksgiving ceremonially to the maple trees.

Dewasentah, Alice Papineau, clan mother of the Eel Clan escorted me back there more than three decades ago.

"This is medicine," she said, handing me a spoonful of new syrup, its color as golden as pure sunlight. "It's a gift from the maple tree. Drink this and you'll be in good health all the year. So we say Nya:weh, thanks to the maple tree."

And that was what I said before tasting that syrup.

"Nya:weh. Thank you for this gift."

Maple syrup is the first harvest of the year. To taste it, to drink it, is to feel your body flowing like those trees. The nutrients in that sap are truly beneficial. A spring tonic to cleanse you of all that has built up over the winter. Nowadays, we can actually buy maple water in grocery stores. But though I suppose it's good, it is not the same.

At our Ndakinna Education Center in Greenfield Center, New York, where we teach outdoor awareness and traditional survival skills, we host small groups of college students from several different schools. They spend a week with us, working around the property while we teach classes and provide them with the opportunity to learn about our northeastern Native traditions of survival and respect for the natural world.

One year when we had such a group, we were making maple syrup from trees on our nature preserve. We had a big pot over a gas burner cooking down the sap on the small open-air stage behind the center where we did presentations. We'd planned to turn the burner off that night, but the eager college kids said they'd take care of it for us.

"Okay," my son Jim said. "Just keep a close eye on it."

The next morning when we arrived at the center we found a group of distraught students waiting, heads down like puppies expecting to be disciplined.

"We're so sorry, we are so sorry, we are so sorry," they chanted—a bunch of penitent pilgrims.

They'd been playing video games and forgot all about the cooking sap. Not only had it boiled down to a black mass, it melted through the pan.

Jim took a look out the window.

"So," he said, indicating the small plume of smoke rising from our outdoor stage, "are you going to put out that fire in the floor now?"

That produced another chorus. This time it was "Oh, no! Oh, no! Oh, no!" as they rushed outside to pour water on the smoldering hole in the thick planks.

Jim and I watched their bucket brigade. Then we listened, not saying anything as they kept apologizing.

"It's okay," Jim said when there was a pause in the recrimination chorus. "It's just a pot and a few planks." He paused and then shrugged. "After all, you did not succeed in burning down the Ndakinna Education Center."

That attempt at humor produced another round of mea culpas.

When they paused for breath, Jim looked at them and nodded. "Okay," he said. "Would you feel better if we yelled at you?"

That finally got a smile out of them, and later that day they showed up with a brand-new cooking pot they had purchased for us—twice as good as the one they'd melted.

My favorite traditional story about maple syrup is the one told among our various Algonquin nations—from the Wabanaki of New England to the Anishinabe of the Great Lakes region.

Gluskonba, who made himself from the dust that sprinkled from the hands of the Great Mystery, was the first one to walk around in the shape of a human. He often helped the people and had the power to change things. It is said that he originally made the maple trees so that they would give the people pure maple syrup all year-round. All you had to do was break a twig and pure golden sweetness came dripping out.

But the time came when people stopped doing anything other than drinking maple syrup. They just lay on their backs, drinking maple syrup, grass growing up around them, no crops being grown, their villages falling apart.

When Gluskonba saw this, he was not pleased. He poured water into the tops of the maple trees and the people all sat up, spitting out that water, asking where their sweet drink had gone.

"You have become lazy," Gluskonba said. "This was too easy for you. From now on to get maple syrup you must gather sap, pour it into wooden canoes. You must gather dry wood to make fires and heat stones to drop into the sap and boil it down. It will take forty buckets of sap to get one bucket of syrup. And so that you will remember to appreciate this gift, it will only come once a year when the snow begins to leave."

And so it has been since then.

I've never done the kind of industrial maple sugaring that was perfected at Cornell University during the years I was a student there. It involves green plastic lines, strung from tree to tree, emptying into a collecting tank. Even, in some cases, using a pump to suck the sap out into those lines.

What I do is just the simple stuff. Drill the hole, tap in the spile (a hollow metal spike), hang the bucket or maybe a plastic jug with a lid on it. Then, the next day, I collect the sap from that tree and a dozen others in another bucket that I then carry to the wide, shallow evaporating pan. There I cook the sap down outside over a woodfire—before finishing it off inside the house on the stove.

I never get more than a few quarts a season, but that's enough to share. Maple syrup I made myself was one of the first gifts I gave to my wife, Nicola, when we started dating. Maybe it made a difference. Better ask her.

And, since giving thanks to the maple is part of all our northeastern Native traditions, I say these words today as I walk into the woods, carrying my hand drill, my buckets, and my spiles.

Wliwini for this time of year.
Wliwini for all the maple seasons past.
Wliwini for those that will come.
Wliwini to the Maple, chief of the trees.
Wliwini to Mother Earth.
Wliwini to Father Sun.
Wliwini to this sweet season.

Chickadee singing
a new song for this morning
everything waking

First pussy willows
white buds on dark branches
replacing the snow

FALLING

Falling. That's what I was doing last week, just after Valentine's Day.

But not in love. Literally falling. An unseasonably warm day in February had been followed by an evening drop in temperature. I stepped out of my car, walked around the back, then . . . Wheee! And I was in the midst of what was doomed to be a failed attempt at levitation.

Oops, forgot one little detail. I'd been eating a banana. Excellent source of potassium after working out. And as I walked across what looked to be clear concrete but was actually glossed with a transparent film of ice, I tossed that banana peel just as I stepped. Ergo, in a new twist on the oldest slapstick gag in the book, I slipped not on but because of a banana peel.

As I was falling, I was also in the process of being reminded by the universe that nothing should ever be taken for granted. Not even the earth beneath our feet.

Pause that mental video whilst I remain in full doomed flight. Note that, first of all, I did not have the presence of mind to cry out shazam! (Though another, monosyllabic comment on my condition did exit my lips, a word starting with that same letter—not that the magic word that transformed Billy Batson, lame newspaper boy into the crimson-suited crusader for justice once known as Captain Marvel.)

Not that shouting "Shazam" would have helped me. After all, I'd tried it before.

I was seven then and addicted to comic books. I was also being bullied in school. I decided then that it was time for desperate measures.

Historical footnote: "Shazam," for those with less image-addled childhoods than mine, was the first acronym I ever learned. It stood for the seven mighty heroes whose powers were transmitted by a bolt of lightning when that word was uttered. Solon (whoever the heck he was) for wisdom, Hercules (knew him) for strength, Atlas (guy holding up the globe, got it), Zeus (king of the Greek gods), and so on.

I knew that others had probably tried it before me. But they weren't Billy Batson. After all, only the truly worthy would it work for. Someone devoted to justice. As I surely was, since after evening the score with Vern and Paul and those others who bloodied my nose and broke my glasses, I had my sights set on tossing all the nuclear weapons in the world into the sun and bringing about world peace. (Plus ending the necessity of cowering under my desk once a week with all the other kids in School Number Two. Ah yes, under a desk. The one place where no atomic bombs could find us.) My only uncertainty was whether I would end up as a muscleman in a red leotard or be issued some other primary color.

I fashioned a cape from one of my grandmother's curtains. I climbed to the top of the chicken house in the backyard. I spread out my arms. I looked up to the heavens and took a deep breath.

Shazam! I cried in what I imagined to be a mighty voice as I leaned forward and let myself fall—eyes closed and teeth clenched just in case it didn't work. I did not want to see it if I hit the ground fifteen feet below. Amazingly, I did not hit the ground. I opened my eyes. I was suspended in midair, my arms held out as if in flight.

This really wor . . . I thought before I heard the sound of cloth ripping as the nail that had caught on my bedroom-curtain cape tore through and I went plummeting down. In the first major fall that I remember. When I not only saw the ground as I hit it, but also ate a big mouthful of it—replete with chicken feed and other unmentionable debris as our Rhode Island reds scattered in panic. And, though not transmogrified into a superhero, I was a bit more like Billy Batson for a week or so after. Lame.

End of flashback numero uno.

I've now, in the millisecond that has elapsed, progressed another inch toward the unforgiving pavement. The image of my grandfather losing his footing on the ice in front of our general store at the age of eighty-three and shattering his hip is by now accompanying me. As well as other more unwanted snapshots.

The time while fishing on the North Branch that a rock gave way underfoot as I made my way down a steep bank. Resulting in my ending up twenty feet below splayed out on top of a midstream boulder, watching my pole float away downstream and feeling like the Warner Brothers cartoon character Wile E. Coyote after being let down yet again by the Acme Company.

Then there was the New Year's Eve party, attended by an assemblage of acquaintances from Yaddo taking a break from the nearby artists colony in Saratoga—folk singer buddies, a number of Native friends, and several visiting African writers from Nigeria whom I'd included in the literary magazine I published back then, *The Greenfield Review*. After drinking way too much, I had decided at two a.m. that the view of the world from the top of a platform built forty feet up in a basswood tree would be especially interesting during the sleet storm then in progress. After watching the beam from the flashlight I'd been holding plummet to the ground like a shooting star, folksinger Bruce (Utah) Phillips ventured out to find me on my knees spitting blood into the snow.

"Joe, are there any internal injuries?"

"No, but I bit my dang tongue and I can't find my glasses."

That, lesson learned, was the end of my drinking.

Getting back to my latest fortunate fall . . .

Whomp. I hit the ground. That whomp was followed by a nearly instantaneous thwack as my head whiplashed back after the initial impact to the middle of my shoulders. Resulting in the brief appearance of a few new stars in the firmament.

I was not knocked out. Thick heads and heavy bones are found in both the European and the Indigenous branches of my family tree. Neanderthal roots, mayhap. But I did remain there for a moment taking stock of the situation. What hurt? My lower back. Not much. More from twisting in midair than from hitting the ground. Back of my head? Not that bad either. Hardly a headache. I'd only feel the pulled muscle in my side twenty-four hours later when it locked up like a nasty little fist in the middle of a Brazilian jiujitsu roll.

I sat up, sliding off the ice as I did so. Hand reaching back to the drier ground inside the garage as I did a fairly respectable technical stand up. And said thank you to my five decades in martial arts, Alliance jiujitsu in particular, because I'd instinctively twisted as I fell so that I landed not on a hip or an elbow but instead in the middle of my back, both arms extended to slap out on the pavement. And also because I was wearing my black Alliance hoodie, which absorbed some of the impact as the back of my skull contacted the concrete.

If there's no way to avoid it, knowing how to go with it
may be the best way. As well as finding at least a little humor
and maybe even a lesson or two from . . .

Falling.

Black ice underfoot
sends me sprawled out on my back
looking up at clouds

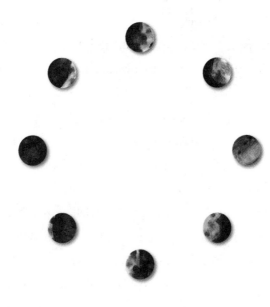

CEGWALIKA

FROG MOON

I BRAKE FOR TOADS

That's what the sticker on the back bumper of my car reads. And I do that whenever I can. Not just for toads but frogs of all species and sizes. I slow down, even stop.

Cegwalika.

That is how we say it in the Abenaki Indian language of my ancestors. "Many Frogs Moon" is what those words mean. And, boy, is it accurate on this wet July evening. They are springing out from the grassy roadside onto the shiny surface of a wet road that resembles black rivers.

From the first rains of April, the Frog Moon, as my Old People called it, on through the warm days of September, the

Moon of Changing, you'll see them risking their lives like this. Leaping, live drops of rain.

It makes me hate to travel major highways when it's raining during those warm season months. At sixty-five miles an hour, I won't be able to stop or swerve to avoid them without endangering my own life or lives in other vehicles. And I know what I'll see the next day when the sun returns if I travel these same roads—crows picking crushed amphibian remains from that dark surface of sacrifice to the gods of human travel.

Such warm and rainy nights have been all too common this year. Last week there were so many of those small green and brown leapers that it took me half an hour to travel the distance it normally would take only ten minutes to cover. Time well spent, though.

Today as I slowed to avoid the spring-loaded leaps of leopard frogs, stopped to get out and relocate the toads that too often persist in holding their ground in the middle of the road, I thought of Swift Eagle. I always do at such times.

Swifty, as his friends called him, was a Santo Domingo Pueblo/Jicarilla Apache elder who befriended me in the 1970s, not long after I'd returned to the United States following three years of teaching in Africa. We traded visits back and forth between his home in Schroon Lake where he and his wife, Chi-Chi, worked at a tourist attraction called Frontier Town. His son Powhatan's trailer was in mobile home park just up the road from us, and the old house in Greenfield Center, where I'd been raised by my grandparents. Back then Pow had a little Native crafts shop on Broadway in Saratoga Springs. That shop was where I first met Swifty in 1970, and our new friendship led to the first of many expeditions up to Schroon Lake.

I'd begun to have a little success as a writer then, was getting invitations to do poetry readings and performances. Swifty liked the songs and poems I was writing.

"Any time you want me to come along with you, Joe," he would say, "you just give this little bird a call."

So I did just that whenever I had a gig in our Adirondack Mountains region. It became a regular thing for the two of us. Once or twice a month I'd pick him up at his home. As we drove, he'd tell me stories, and we performed together— audiences loving the way he played his red cedar flute to accompany my poems, his high lilting notes lifting my words.

One July day when I picked him up the sky was heavy with dark clouds.

"Looks like it's going to pour," I said, as he climbed into the front seat.

"We will have to be careful," he said. "Verrry careful, Joe."

"Uh, yes," I agreed, not quite sure what he meant. But soon after that rain began to come down. It hit so hard at first that it was as if a heavy veil had been dropped around us. It was only six p.m., but even with the headlights and the wipers on high, it was almost impossible to see. We were the only car on the road. No one else was crazy enough to drive in that sort of weather.

It finally let up when we turned onto Route 2, a road that runs through Blue Ridge to Newcomb where we'd pick up 28N, the same corkscrewed-through-the-mountains route where Vice President Theodore Roosevelt made his famous Adirondack wagon ride in 1901 after getting word that President William McKinley was dying.

I was concerned that we were running late. The Adirondack Lakes Center for the Arts in Blue Mountain Lake was more than an hour's drive away, and the rain was slowing us down. I always try to arrive early whenever I perform. It's not fair to audiences and event organizers to keep them waiting.

So, when the rain let up and I could see clearly again, I pushed down on the gas.

"No," Swifty said. "Slow up, Joe."

Huh?

But I did as he asked.

"Stop!" he said.

His voice was so urgent that I did so without a second's hesitation. The car skidded a little as it came to a halt, but Swifty paid that no mind. He had the door open and was halfway out before it stopped sliding. He trotted around front, bent down, and stood up with a smile on his face. And a fat, unharmed toad in his hand.

"See," he said.

He walked over to the road edge, bent down, carefully released it, came back to the car, and climbed in.

"Okay, Joe," he said. "We go."

But not far. A hundred yards farther and then—

"Stop!"

This time it was not a toad, but a frog, one that didn't let him pick it up, but was herded by his open hands to safety into the tall roadside grass.

I was moved. But I was also worried.

How long were we going to keep this up?

Two more stops. More amphibian rescue missions. Then three stops, four, five.

The rain had almost stopped, but our suicidal little wet-skinned friends had not. There were far too many more frogs and toads on the road ahead of us. They were clearly visible for a hundred yards ahead, easier to see as the mist rose from the road in swirling veils of white.

We were never going to get there.

"Swifty," I said, as he was opening his door yet again, "we've got to be somewhere."

He turned back toward me. "They have to be somewhere too," he said, his voice slow and patient. Then he smiled. "You will see. It will aa-aall be all right."

From then on, it was both of us getting out each time we stopped. I don't know how many small lives we saved that day. But for some reason my anxiety had left me by the time the clouds had vanished and there were no longer any little creatures to be seen on the blacktop. The road ahead of us was clear, and though we were still this side of Newcomb and certain to be very, very late, there was a smile on my face as I drove.

Swifty was saying something.

"What's that?" I asked.

"Don't worry, Joe," he said again.

"How's that?" I asked.

"Because we're here," he answered.

Huh?

We were. Somehow, we were already at the point where Routes 28N and 28 intersect. The lake was on our right, the Adirondack Center for the Arts a quarter mile farther on our left. The last thing I'd noticed, back when I first heard Swifty say, "Don't worry, Joe," was that we hadn't even reached Long Lake. We'd been more than twenty miles away.

As I pulled into the parking lot behind the building, I looked at my watch. We were ten minutes early. It didn't make sense.

Swifty was saying something again. I looked over at him.

"You see, Joe," he repeated, "I told you it would aa-aall be all right."

"We're on time," I said.

Swift Eagle shook his head. "Joe," he replied, "time doesn't really exist."

Did it happen that way? All I can say is that's how I remember it.

And then I wrote a poem about that rainy journey of ours called "Birdfoot's Grampa." It appeared in a book of my own poems a few years later and has since been anthologized more than a hundred times and translated into more than a dozen languages.

Birdfoot's Grampa

The old man
must have stopped our car
two dozen times to climb out
and gather into his hands
the small toads blinded
by our light and leaping
live drops of rain.
The rain was falling,
a mist about his white hair
and I kept saying
you can't save them all
accept it, get back in
we've got places to go.
But, leathery hands full
of wet brown life,
knee deep in the summer
roadside grass,
he just smiled and said
they have places to go too.

There's no direct mention of time in that poem, but for me it works as a sort of time machine. Every time I read that poem, and every time I'm driving through a warm rain, I'm back there again in my old car. Swift Eagle is by my side.

And we are stopping for every frog, every toad. We're both wet. We're both smiling. We're both unworried about getting anywhere on time. What really exists, what truly counts, is not time, but life.

Chorus frogs singing
from the pond in our backyard
here I, here I am

Bull thistle's spiral
reminding us how all things
exist in circles

TADPOLES

I'd planned to plant beans this morning. Thinking poetically, perhaps, of Walden Pond as I did it.

But it's raining. Not a heavy downpour. A thin mist that's felt more than seen. The thousand shades of green glisten from the moisture. A small wind, the exhaled breath of the earth, trembles the white blossoms of the plum trees. A brushstroke of wheat-colored pines needles is spread across the black driveway. So I decide to wait.

Looking around the backyard for another spring task, my eyes stop at the garden pond.

I haven't brought the big koi out. They are still in the watering trough in the basement that I use as a winter home for them. Each morning the sound of their splashing greets me as I thump down the red-painted stairs. They swirl and roll at the surface, their mouths open for the dry pellets I offer them.

There's better food for them in this outdoor pool. Yesterday when I looked into its leaf-clogged waters I saw hundreds of black dots with whipping tails—like punctuation marks come to life—feeding on the algae that grows on the green rubber liner. Those tiny ones are the results of the trilling songs I first heard two weeks or so ago. Tadpoles of several sizes, when I look closer. Chorus frogs. Toads. Green frogs. Even a few chubby bullfrog babies.

Those small, metamorphosing swimmers are the reason I'll wait till last night's full moon has shrunk back to a sliver in the sky before introducing my three orange and silver predators back into their warm-season home. Time enough for legs to grow and those amphibious tenants to join their brethren in the trees, under the leaf litter, and in Bucket Pond itself fifty yards down the hill.

The journey they'll be taking transports my mind to another place and time. Quartz Mountain State Park. That's where I was three decades ago.

My friend Lance and I and a group of other artists in various disciplines were there for two weeks to teach at the Oklahoma Summer Arts Institute, a program that brought 200 carefully chosen high school students from throughout Oklahoma to nurture their creativity.

Quartz Mountain is in the town called Lone Wolf, Oklahoma, in the ancient Wichita Range—not far from the Rainy Mountain that N. Scott Momaday wrote about. A part of Oklahoma where in 1874 the Red River War was fought. Where Lone Wolf and other leaders of the Southern Plains nations tried to drive out the buffalo hunters who were wiping out the sacred herds that were life and culture to the Kiowas, the Comanches, the Cheyennes, Arapahos, Wichitas, and others who banded together to resist.

I'm pretty sure it was Lance's idea to climb the tallest mountain there with our students.

"They need to see the dawn," Lance said. And I agreed.

I love to climb mountains. But it's not to reach the highest height, to conquer the peak. Nor to say I've scaled the Matterhorn or Kilimanjaro or Everest—where the frozen bodies of climbers who perished along the way are actually seen as trail markers. That kind of counting coup on the landscape doesn't interest me. It's what you feel up there in the space between earth and sky, the way a mountain sunrise enters your breath, your heart.

King Mountain rises 2,400 feet to its summit. Lance and I hiked up it first to make sure we knew the route to follow as we led our kids through the dark before first light the next day.

When we reached the top, which I'd expected to be bone dry like much of the high places of the Wichita Range, I got a surprise. There was water there. A bathtub-sized depression in the bedrock held a pool three feet deep, filled from a recent cloudburst. But that wasn't all.

"Check this out, brother," Lance said, pointing with his lips for me to look beneath the surface.

I leaned closer. The pool was swarming with hundreds of tadpoles. I peered around us. There was no way a frog could survive for long up there. Just a few scrubby plants, ink-blotch patterns of lichen on the gray stones. Down farther below there was moister habitat, but it was distant, half a mile or more. Western chorus frogs, no doubt. The little inch-long striped frogs of the prairies. In my mind came the image of them hopping up the trail during that rain. Then this temporary pool becoming a breeding place filled with their songs. *Prrreeep, prreeep, prrreeep* as they mated and then left their egg masses to hatch.

I looked a question at Lance, who nodded.

"Yup," he said. "That's what happened."

We didn't say a word about that small mountaintop miracle to our students when we set out the next day at four a.m. Let it be a surprise for them as it was for us.

It wasn't an easy climb for some of our kids, despite the flashlights we let them use. Scrabbling over stones, breathing hard, tripping now and then. A few barked knuckles and bruised knees, but they all completed the climb. Even Etheleen Poolaw, a slightly out of shape but determined young Kiowa-Apache girl whose first poems had showed a depth of emotion that touched everyone in our workshop. Even though she had a few extra pounds holding her back, she had the determination of a woman warrior.

"I ... am ... going ... to make ... it ... even if ... I die trying!" she panted, refusing anyone's help as she struggled up the last hundred yards.

There was just a hint of light in the east as Lance and I lit the fire. It had died down to coals by the time the horizon started to glow red and gold. We sprinkled dried cedar needles on the embers as Lance showed our students how to bathe themselves in that healing smoke, cupping hands to waft it up to faces, to arms and legs, to hearts.

We all sat there for a timeless time as the great day star lifted, the shadows ran across the land, and the songs of birds rose: meadowlarks, blackbirds, sparrows, a western cardinal from farther down the mountain.

Then Lance and I looked at each other.

"Come on," he said, standing up, "we got something to show you."

We weren't the first to reach that indentation in the mountaintop. Which was all that we found when we joined the circle of young writers peering down into the barely moist stone bowl.

No pool. No tadpoles.

My heart sank. Oh, no, I was thinking. It dried up before we got here, and they all died.

"Look at this," Etheleen said.

As we turned in her direction, we saw what she was looking at. An inch-long frog, its moist back marked with three broad stripes, the tiniest bit of a tadpole tail not yet absorbed back into its body.

"There are more of them here," someone else said.

"And here."

"And here."

It was true, there were small frogs all around us. We had to walk with the greatest care to avoid stepping on them. And all of them were now moving in the same direction. Toward the trail we had used to climb up.

They were hopping all around us as we went down King Mountain. All around us the pulse of life was flowing back down from the dry stone peak. Continuing a cycle as old as the gifts that are always there for us when we pause to accept them. Held by the earth that always remembers more than the temporary lines marked on maps.

A good memory for both the earth and me as I look out the window and see the rain has stopped now.

Is it really too wet today for me to turn more earth in the raised garden beds? Probably not, but then there are the black flies. The wind that has followed the rain is not quite strong enough to swirl away the black flies that showed up last week—like a switch had been turned on. Right on time—just when the weather is finally warm enough for me to walk about sans shirt and shoes.

Okay, to be honest, I may do that any time of year. I sometimes step out bare chested and barefooted onto the open deck to move through the deliberate steps, strikes, and kicks of a martial arts kata, delighting in the pattern of footprints left behind in a first snow. Or crawl, wearing no more than at my first birth, out of the deep cleansing heat of the sweat lodge to fall backward into the white embrace of a drift. How lovely it is when your body is hot enough to melt down through three feet of blue-shaded snow.

But the freezing seasons are not the time when one can linger long outdoors and still remain among the breathing. Unlike spring when you can lie back on the hill moss, spread out your arms, and close your eyes, unafraid of sleeping.

Until the black flies come swarming in and leave your body covered with red dots where their rasping mouth parts removed your red corpuscles. But who can blame them? The iron in your blood is as necessary for the fulfillment of their life cycle as it is for the female mosquitoes who soon follow, buzzing in your ears as if trying to share some special secret with you.

I'm neither a Buddhist nor a Jain. You'll not find me giving my body to a starving tiger and her young—nor wearing gauze over my face to keep from inhaling and inadvertently ending the life of some small being. So rather than share my vital fluids with those little vampiric flyers, I do my early spring gardening in long sleeves and with a hat equipped with mesh small enough to prevent the penetration of most (but not all) of those various critters labeled as pests.

I don't resent them. I've never wanted to install one of those electric traps that incinerate not just mosquitoes but moths and any other lace-winged night flyer, each sizzling zap that cuts through the night marking another immolation. Nor do I spray the air with any of those chemical mists—that might knock down a few bugs but also are just as efficient at infiltrating your own lungs.

I think of how Tehanetorens, the Mohawk elder whose European name was Ray Fadden, explained it to me decades ago when he decried all the aerial spraying for mosquitoes and the various biochemical campaigns being waged by North Country towns against the black flies. "They're breaking the cycle of life," he said. "All those birds and others that feed on those black flies. What are they going to eat if we get rid of them?"

Why is it that our species always feels it must fix everything? To make it better—briefly—for us at the expense of everything else? I don't have an answer for that, not for anyone other than myself. But there is a phrase in the Abenaki language that was spoken by my ancestors and that lives in the mouths of my grandchildren. *Akwi gamadw8zi*. Which simply means, "You should not complain."

The wind is stronger, fluttering the leaves like a hand stroking the hair of a child, and sweeping away the black flies. A small, warm rain is falling again. The fragrance of the jasmine in my little combination kitchen and dining room is like a counterpoint to the subtler scent of the blossoms from the fruit trees that I inhale as I step outside. Ah, yes.

And I still have not planted those beans.

No, no gardening for me this morning. Time to walk bare headed in the spring rain, remembering tadpoles and smiling.

Cool it, Henry David.

I'll plant beans on another day.

Gold dandelions
push up from the old road's edge
welcoming the sun

KIKAS

MOON OF PLANTING

BUTTERFLIES

As I walk along the dirt road with my dog, Kiki, I notice something in the dry leaves. It looks at first like a leaf itself. Then it slowly unhinges its wings and flutters up. Those small wings seem tattered at first but then I see it's just the pattern, the familiar black-and-gold striped markings of a mourning cloak butterfly.

One of the first butterflies of the spring. One of the first I learn to identify. Maybe just emerged from its pupa or a survivor of the winter that wedged itself under a piece of rough bark like that on a nearby cherry tree.

It lifts up as if to greet me, then flies in a close circle around my legs, one, two three, four times before dropping down to rest for a moment on my left shoe.

As we continue walking, another butterfly, a small white one, flies by so fast I cannot identify it. Then, smaller than a dime, a tiny butterfly, a skipper, lands right in front of me, and I have to stop walking. They are so small that I suspect most people don't even notice them. But this seems to be a morning of butterflies for me.

It's a walk the dog and I make every morning, but this is the first one where I've seen butterflies. Perhaps because I've been thinking of them. But also because such a profusion of flowers has begun to bloom. The yellow colt's foot blossoms have all passed now, transformed into the thin white hair of seeds being scattered by the breeze. But the sun-gold burst of dandelions, the delicate whites and purples of violets, and the pale, glowing blossoms of wild strawberries are reaching up everywhere to be kissed by the sunlight.

All these are sure signs that this is Kikas, the Moon of Planting. Just as are the unfolded leaves of the maple trees. "When them maple leaves," my grandfather used to say, "they're the size of a squirrel's ear. That's the time to start putting in your corn."

My grandfather's voice seems to come back to me most often whenever I work the garden, or even think about working it. Our morning walk done, I lean over to break off one of the first sprouts of asparagus from the new raised bed—new because it's only a decade planted. It's not half a century old like the one half a mile from here that my old neighbor Otto Plaug—who passed at the age of 105—dug in at his garden's edge. As I chew that first taste of harvest, there's a small grain of earth that crunches in my teeth as I eat it. But I don't spit that bit of soil out, just swallow it remembering Grampa Jesse's words seventy years gone as he handed me a just-pulled carrot that he didn't wash but just wiped clean between his brown fingers. "Everbody's got t' eat a ton of dirt in their life."

Old men, old garden beds, old memories . . . new leaves, new butterflies, and the promise of new harvests each season of planting.

> White blossoms glisten
> in the plum tree's top branches
> swaying in the wind

MOUNTAIN LIONS

It's a warm spring morning, the ground moist after last night's rain. A good morning for tracking, I think, as I follow the old dirt road that passes over two small streams before it dead ends a mile past our cabin.

And, sure enough, in the mud at the edge of the second narrow brook that runs down from Little Bucket Pond I find fresh cat tracks. Too large for a domestic feline. I can feel it watching me from the concealment of the brush farther downstream.

Bobcat. Not mountain lion. None of those large cats are around here anymore, though they are still in the memory of people my age. *Felis concolor*. That's the Latin name I learned for it when I was a wildlife conservation major at Cornell University years ago. But that's not its only name in English. No animal I can think of has more common names. Puma, cougar, panther, painter, catamount, ghost cat. Those are only a few of its appellations.

I love big cats. No, that doesn't mean I want to be like the Tiger King, a slightly deranged TV personality with a caged array of apex predators in the background. Or someone whose obituary reads "Killed by his 600-pound pet pussycat."

No thanks, Siegfried and Roy.

Mountain lions are big enough for me. They connect to all our Indigenous cultures here in North America south of the Arctic. In pre-European times they were everywhere. All the way through the Americas, from the Canadian Yukon to the Tierra del Fuego.

In our Wabanaki traditions, when there were giant animals before the humans came, our culture hero Gluskonba called all the animals together. He was worried that they might harm the human beings who were soon to arrive. He asked each of them what they would do when they first saw a human. Some said they would eat the people or tear them apart. So he changed the biggest, fiercest ones to make them less dangerous. He shrank down the bear, the giant moose, and the most dangerous one of all back then—the vicious, terrible Mikwe, the enormous red squirrel.

But just when he thought he was finished, Gluskonba noticed one more sizable creature hanging back. Hiding behind a big pine tree with only its tail sticking out was the mountain lion. So Gluskonba crept up quietly and grabbed its tail. But Mountain Lion leaped then and pulled so hard that it yanked its tail out of Gluskonba's grasp. However, its tail got stretched out so that it became as long as its body, black at the end where Gluskonba had grabbed it. Thus our name for the mountain lion is Bitahlo—Long Tail.

Just as in that story, Bitahlo still has a way of trying to stay out of sight, sneaking up on prey. In fact, if you are ever in mountain lion country, though you may not see it, one is probably watching you.

As I'm writing this, there's a good chance that my older son, Jim, is being watched by a mountain lion right now. A professional tracker who has written books on the subject, he is currently out West doing research for a new book on grizzly bears, tracking them in Montana, where the bears' range is shared with cougars.

I would not go so far as to say that our Indigenous people were afraid of mountain lions. After all, we did hunt them on occasion—though respecting them was more often the case. And what hunting we did was to make use of its skin for clothing, its teeth and claws for necklaces or talismans—borrowing the big cat's power.

Power, indeed. Even a small mountain lion is a lot stronger than most human beings. Generally, of course, it will not take a person straight on. Not in most cases. Sneak up behind, leap, take your neck in its mouth with its strong teeth just as it might grab a deer. One quick twist and snap! Just like that deer, you're dead.

There's a giant glacial erratic on the trail that leads up over Glass Factory Mountain to Lake Desolation. That mammoth stone, big as a small cabin, is called Panther Rock. The story is that the last mountain lion in our area was shot by a hunter who saw it crouching up there about to leap on him.

It's a story that makes me sad. In fact, though our mountain slopes are heavily wooded again, there was a time less than century ago when clear-cut logging and overhunting had resulted in even the deer being so rare that when one was shot and brought into Windsor Cote's general store in Greenfield Center, folks came from miles around to marvel at it.

Now, the woods are back. And so are many of the animals that were missing in my grandfather's time. Not just deer and bear, but even moose. And, just about every year there are reports of mountain lions being seen. A few years back, a juvenile mountain lion was shot and killed near here. And the year before that, two adult mountain lions were shot near Corinth, only fifteen miles away. But all of those were identified as captive animals escaped from private owners. Virtually every sighting hereabouts of what people think is a mountain lion has either been unverified or turned out to be a bobcat.

Most of my own experience with mountain lions has been with ones no longer in the wild. Koda is the prime example. There is a picture of her with me on the back of my book *Seeing the Circle*. A 100-pound South American mountain lion, she'd been imported into the United States in the illegal—and quite frankly evil—exotic pet trade. Her claws had been removed and there was no way she could go back into the wild. But a group called Animal Awareness, which was federally licensed and used captive animals for educational purposes, adopted Koda after she was taken from her former owner. They worked with us for several years, bringing her and other educational animals such as foxes and wolves to our Ndakinna Education Center.

Koda loved those visits. Being walked through the woods of our nature preserve, a leash attached to her harness, made her happy. The only times I saw her upset were when it was time for Animal Awareness to leave and she was being put back into her travel cage—and when the photographer who took the picture that appears on the back of *Seeing the*

Circle snapped a few too many photos and she snarled so threateningly at him that he referred to her as "that thing with all the teeth!"

Another of the photos he took shows her sitting behind me with her paws on my shoulder and her head poised near my neck. Yes, the pose a mountain cat takes when it has leaped on a deer and is about to break its neck. Which she could have done. A 100-pound cougar can easily drag a 700-pound elk carcass up a tree.

I'll never forget what happened when one of our instructors, a muscular young man who weighed more than 160 pounds (I'll call him Frank) asked if he could take Koda's leash and walk her.

"Okay," my son Jim said, "but . . ."

Jim was about to explain what I'd been taught many years before by a California Native elder named Coyote. When you first start to walk a leashed mountain lion, do it straddling the animal. That's the way a mother mountain lion controls her cubs. But Jim never finished what he was about to say.

"I got it," Frank said. "She won't get away. See, I'm wrapping the leash around my wrist."

And that was when a chipmunk ran out of the woods farther down the path. Koda took off like a shot. She dragged Frank behind her like a flag in the wind for a good hundred feet before the lucky chipmunk managed to find safety by scooting off the path through a tangle of multifloral rose bushes and into a stone wall.

There's only one time when I encountered a mountain lion in the wild. A decade and a half ago one crossed my path as I was walking to a friend's mailbox, at the foot of the driveway that led to her house up in the mountains fifteen miles above Boulder, Colorado. The mountain wind was in my face and so the mountain lion couldn't catch my scent. I think I saw it at the same time it noticed me. It paused, one foot up, and looked at me the way all cats have a way of looking at humans. Pretty much the same way your tabby peruses a mouse.

Of all the creatures on this earth none like the taste of our human flesh more than any cat of any size. Every year tigers still feast on hapless farmers in parts of India. I was seven when I read the book *Maneaters of Kumaon* by Jim Corbett, a British hunter who killed almost as many tigers as the hundreds of people they devoured.

But it's not just really big cats who smack their lips at the thought of long pig. There are tabloid stories about some elderly cat lady, all alone in her little apartment with her two dozen cats who were kept well fed till she had that stroke or heart attack. When, a week later, the emergency crew broke down the door, because neighbors had not seen her for a while and were complaining about the smell, do I have to tell you what they found? Despite her demise, her kitties had found a handy source of protein.

Getting back to that mountain lion and me, I imagined what might be going on in its head as it eyed me.

Turn around, it may have been thinking. *Try to run away. I like a challenge.*

And what was I thinking?

Number one thought was that I was glad to see it was a pretty big cougar. Most human deaths by way of mountain lions are caused by cats younger than two years old. Maybe as small as eighty pounds and recently kicked out by their mother who has a new litter to care for. Not yet smart enough to know that hunting people, easy as it may seem, can only bring brief satisfaction before being brought down itself.

Number two thought was that at six feet two inches tall and just over two hundred pounds, I might have seemed a little big. The two humans killed recently in Colorado—not that far from the very slope where I stood—were half my size. One was a slender mountain biker bent over to repair a tire. The other was a jogger intent on conquering a hill and not looking over her shoulder.

In the old days, back in my eastern mountains when my Old People walked through *ktsi kpiwi*, the big forest, where Bitahlo, the long tailed one, might pounce out in ambush after we had passed, on the back of our packs we fastened tight two sharp stakes. A leaping lion would land on those if it tried to take us down from behind.

I have on my wall above my desk a tapestry telling the story of a tiger who killed a hunter. It was given to me by a Hmong artist I met in Denver. In their high jungles of Southeast Asia when walking through places where there were tigers, Hmong might wear a mask with painted eyes wide open on the back of their heads. Thus, it seemed they were aware of anything behind them.

Thought number three was that running from a cougar is never a good idea. Nor is making yourself small and playing dead as you might do in the case of a bear attack. Playing dead just gives a big cat that much more time to decide which part of your anatomy to start snacking on first. So, there was no way on God's green earth that I was going to turn and flee up the steep gravel driveway that led back to the house a hundred yards off around the bend.

I looked at it as it looked at me. Then I smiled and raised a hand.

"Not today," I said, "go find you a mule deer."

And, just like that, it turned its gaze away from me, continued on across the road, and disappeared into a downhill maze of boulders and brush.

I stood up from where I'd been crouching to study those feline tracks and been taken by memory. Bobcat or not, I'd felt the hair on the back of my neck standing up as I leaned over the stream. The small rush of adrenaline brought on by recollection and imagination had been bracing . . . and a reminder.

I looked at the forest around me and nodded my head.

"Thank you," I said, "for reminding me that we humans are not the most important things in this world."

Pine needles turning
back into brown forest soil
piled up by my rake

SPRING RAIN

The spring rain is so light this morning that it's almost mist. Just barely visible, as it falls on the bare skin of my arms, small reflective drops form on the hair of my wrist.

It's good to walk in the rain on a day such as this. Neither too cold nor too hot, feeling this life-giving moisture becoming part of my breath.

One small basswood tree overarching the trail already has leaves as large as both of my hands held together, spread out.

There's a place along its slender trunk where something, perhaps the falling of that larger pine branch on the ground below it, tore along the trunk, disclosing the inner bark of the tree. That bark is supple, resilient. When it is stripped out, it's stronger than an average rope. In the past it was used to make cordage and was woven into baskets. I've done both. Wigbimezi is the tree's Abenaki name. Basket Tree.

I remember Maurice Dennis showing me how strong a piece of basswood can be. He took a length about eight feet long, looped it over the top of the branch of a maple, and tied a knot in it. Then he said, "Here's a swing, Joe."

And it truly was. It held my 200 pounds as I sat in it and swung back and forth while he continued working on the pole he was carving, working on the shape of a turtle with its thirteen plates on its back. One for each moon, he told me. And it was from his words that my first published picture book, coauthored with my friend Jonathan London, arose.

Just one small tree . . . and seeing it brings so many stories to me. It's like that with everything around me. Everything has its own tale to tell or at least to help us tell.

Like the stones I see on the dead-end dirt road that passes our cabin. Each morning I pick one up, feel its smoothness in my hand. Some of them clearly were lithic tools, fitting so well between fingers and wrist that I know they were used for scraping or pounding. Others just have a familiar feeling as if they were meant to be carried for a while. Beside the turnaround at the end of the road I have a small pile of them, each stone chosen for its color, its smoothness, or just the way it seemed to indicate it wanted to accompany me on my walk.

Some of those stones glisten, almost as bright as glass, even when they are not moistened by rain. They have quartz in them, mica and feldspar. I feel blessed each day by them. What a privilege it is to have so many stones to see, to pick up and carry for a while. Though some seem to want to just be put back down and left where I saw them at the road's edge. While others in the middle of the road just want to be removed from where the tires of all-terrain vehicles kick them up and sometimes break them.

As I look down, I see something else. It's a feather. Tip banded with rusty red, the rest a sandy cinnamon color, I know where it came from. It was dropped by the red-tailed hawk that nests not far from here. I've seen it and its mate circling high in the sky, heard their calls that Walt Whitman described so well as a barbaric yawp. Though, to be perfectly honest, the real barbarians are not the hawks. As another late, great Walt (cartoonist Walt Kelly) put it through his philosopher possum Pogo, "We have met the enemy and they is us."

The rain is letting up a bit now. The sky turning light, high wisps of cloud scudding across it. Perhaps the sun will break through, and I'll see off toward the east the arc of a rainbow. Managwon, "The Arch on Its Own" is our old Abenaki word for it. In the Old Testament story of Noah, the rainbow was a sign. It still is today. Not just an emblem of survival but also a reminder that we need to take better care of the earth or it will be the fire next time.

Although not today—as the rain keeps spattering on my cap.

There's no rainbow yet, but I don't mind waiting
for one.

Bark peels from the birch
popping free all on its own
as the light rain falls

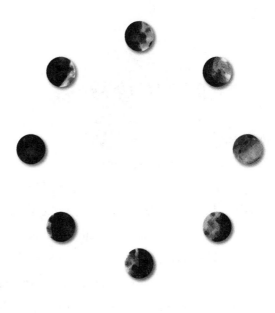

NOKKAHIGAS

MOON OF HOEING

KO-KO-LEEYO-KWAY!

I'm outside just before sunrise when I hear it.

I put down the hoe and pause on my way to the garden as it provides the soundtrack to the first light sifting through the pines downhill. The rooster's challenge to the new day. It's a high combative tone that cuts through the hundred yards between our cabin and the Sullivans' house.

The sunrise is especially bright here, just as the sunsets and the stars are. We're free of the halogen streetlights of such cities as Albany, lights that unshade the sky thirty-five miles south of our Adirondack foothills. We're also free of anti-farming zoning restrictions, which made it possible for our neighbors to start keeping a small flock of those birds whose ancestors were the territorial jungle fowl of Southeast Asia.

Ko-ko-leeyo-kway!

Each morning that sound rings through the early hours. And unlike some who grew up unaccustomed to that clarion call, I welcome it. I like where it takes me.

It's amazing, isn't it, how something that touches only one of your senses—a distinctive scent, a certain sound—can take over the neural pathways in your brain and transport you to another place, another time?

That is why I heard that cock crow not in the old English onomatopoeic form of Cock-a-doodle-do! but the way it sounds to the ears of a certain West African tribal nation whose homeland I once shared. The Anlo people of southeastern Ghana who live on the fifty-mile-long arm of sand called the Keta Peninsula that stretches into the Gulf of Guinea.

It was 1966 when my feet first touched African earth. It's embarrassing to think how young I was then and how much I thought I knew. True, I had my BA from Cornell and my master's degree from Syracuse University. And I'd marched with Martin Luther King into Jackson, Mississippi, taken part in sit-ins, read poetry against the Vietnam War with Robert Bly. And rather than merely protest against social injustice (and the craziness we sensed building in America at that time, when some of the brightest of my friends were losing themselves in the anarchy of drugs) my wife, Carol, and I had decided to try to do something useful. We'd volunteered and joined a program called Teachers for West Africa. (Not the Peace Corps, which had been leery of my activist past.) Two years of teaching English language and English literature in a secondary school were ahead of me—and then volunteering for a third year to see my students through their O- and A-Level exams.

Those years in Africa are more deserving of a book than a brief essay like this. So I'll simply say that I learned more than I taught—and that my best teachers were men and women whose own educations were not in schools, but from their lives—as fishermen, as market women, as traditional priests and makers of drum songs, as people who were even on the fringes of their own society and labeled as mad. And I'll also say that I learned as much about my own nation as I did about Africa. It was in Ghana that I saw more clearly my own identity as a Native American person in an America that marginalized and misunderstood Indians.

For now, though, let me just reminisce about that morning wake-up call the rooster offered me today before I opened my eyes. Because when I opened them, I wondered for a moment why it was so cool in the room, why the fan was not turning over the bed, and where the three geckos with their suction cup toes, those little house lizards that always went about their morning rounds catching insects on the concrete ceiling overhead, had gone.

Oh, wait, that was more than four decades ago.

But even so, as I lay there in bed knowing I was long years and miles away from Keta Secondary School, where the wind from the nearby seas often carried the sounds of the fishermen chanting as they pulled their long blue nets, a part of me expected to hear another sound. Someone tapping on my door and calling out in the Ewe the Kaw-kaw-kaw that visitors would use to announce their at times shockingly early arrival at my threshold. Although, since our door was never locked, some of my students and neighbors would dispense with both knock and greeting and just walk in to take a seat on the couch. We'd walk out of our bedroom and find someone—or several someones—sitting there, browsing through the photo albums we left out. After our first week in Ghana we got over the initial shock and learned both to answer the greeting of "Morning, morning, eh fon" (forgive the phonetic spelling) with "Morning, morning, meh fon, wo ha eh fon . . . " and also to make sure we were at least partially attired before venturing out into that communal living room.

One of our first morning visitors was Mr. Logah-Williams, who lived in a nearby compound and raised some of those chickens that greeted the Ghanaian dawn so vociferously. Impeccably dressed in neatly pressed trousers and a long-sleeved white shirt, erect as a flagpole in his posture, he had grown up during the colonial period that ended with Ghana's becoming the first sub-Saharan Black nation to gain its independence from England. English was and remains the national language of Ghana—both a legacy of that colonial period and a logical choice in a nation with many Indigenous languages. But the English spoken in Ghana and Nigeria and numerous other former colonies by most people was often pronounced with an un-British accent and colored by colloquialisms that grew out of the original tongues—such as saying, "I am coming," to mean, "I will be coming back" or doubling words for emphasis, as in "small small."

But not Mr. Logah-Williams, whose hyphenated last name accentuated the British influence on his upbringing. The English he spoke was as precise as that which his white Cambridge graduate teachers had spoken in the 1930s.

"A fine morning to you, sir," he said, firmly taking my hand and ending the shake with the traditional Anlo snap of our fingers. "I have come to visit because it has been brought to my attention that we have a shared interest."

"Ah," I said, "and that would be. . . ?"

"Poultry," he replied. "I am been informed by your estimable headmaster Mr. Matanawui that, like myself, you are aficionado of fowl."

"Oh," I said. "I see." And because I did not have the heart to tell him that my interest—clearly misheard—was in poetry and not poultry, we then spent what was for him a delightful hour discussing the pros and cons of such American breeds as the Rhode Island red and the Plymouth Rock as compared to, for example the Derbyshire redcap and the Scots grey.

All of which, in the Anlo region of Ghana, say:

Ko-ko-leeyo-kway!

Rain filling the bowl
of the bird bath by the shed
each drop one soft note

SMILING JOE

As I looked at my increasingly lined face in the mirror on this final day of April, I just couldn't keep from chuckling.

"Smiling Joe Bruchac," I said, "no matter how many years pass, you never lose your looks. Young or old, you're still just as ugly."

Smiling Joe.

That was one of my nicknames in high school.

It's a name that might have been an echo from a comic strip popular in those days: *The Adventures of Smilin' Jack*, who was a daredevil pilot. But whatever its genesis, it's a nickname that came back to me this morning.

I've actually had several reminders of that nickname over the past year. Which made me think it might still be appropriate to some degree. My young friend and semi-scion Eric Jenks mentioned it when he gave me his Christmas present, a photo of myself just about to lock up in a jiujitsu bout at the New York Open Tournament.

"You smiled through that whole match, Joe," Eric said.

Guilty as charged. But it is hard not to smile when you are having fun, including while you are in midair after being body-locked, halfway through the process of being suplexed (more like souffléd in my case) by an extremely competent opponent twenty years younger and twenty pounds heavier. (With no one in my seven-decades-old bracket or my 200-pound weight class, I'd decided to move down and up rather than pick up an unearned medal. Ah . . . to get picked up in turn by Tracey, a former championship power lifter who had been sponsored by his entire small town of Paradise in Muhlenberg County, Kentucky. (Great song, John Prine, and nice takedown, Tracey!)

Smiling Joe.

It was the spring of my junior year in high school when I first earned that name. I hadn't yet "gotten my growth," as my Grampa Jesse used to say. The five inches in height and thirty pounds or so in weight had not yet been added on that would transform me from geek to jock in one head-spinning six-month span. And I wasn't all that popular yet—a hick kid from the country with an irritatingly large vocabulary, a penchant for poetry, and, to be honest, an underlying shyness.

On that particular spring day, during the lunch hour break when we were allowed to leave the school, I had trailed along with a bunch of other boys two blocks down Lake Avenue to Lee's.

There's a parking lot and a restaurant now where that little general store—named by Mr. Goodwin for his son—used to be. Lee's was a popular hangout, not just for the candy and soda and other snacks we could buy there, but also for Mr. Goodwin himself. He was like a younger version of my grandfather, a storeowner who both tolerated and liked teenagers and had a great sense of humor. His wisecracks were wry and amusing, but never hurtful.

I'm not sure what I was smiling about, nervousness in all likelihood, as I sat on the steps of the store that day. But another bigger kid named Red, who had a reputation as a bully, took note of my smile and that it might be construed as being aimed in his general direction. He stepped up to me.

"What are you smiling at?"

I said the first thing that came into my head. The wrong thing, of course.

"Nothing."

"You sayin' I'm nothin', you little creep?"

I realized right away what was happening. What should have occurred next was either that I would back down and be shown up as a yellow-bellied coward (a phrase popularized by the western TV shows of that time), or that I would get the crap knocked out of me.

For some reason that just made my grin get bigger. I stood up and let my vocabulary take over.

"No, quite the contrary, my good fellow. I am relatively sure that you are something. Though whether it is Neanderthal or *Pithecanthropus erectus* is somewhat beyond my powers of deduction."

It was almost a knockout punch. Or at least the equivalent of a jab. It made Red step back for a moment and shake his head while he tried to decipher what had just been said.

But then, recovering from my verbal assault, he grabbed my wrist and tried to twist it. Without success. Although I'd never been in a fight before—if that was what was happening—I was stronger than I looked. The baggy clothes my beloved grandmother dressed me in disguised the fact that even at 150 pounds and five feet nine inches tall I wasn't soft. My favorite pastime back then was to roam the woods behind our house and climb to the top of the tallest trees I could find.

I looked at Red and he looked at me. Then he grabbed my arm with two hands. Curious about what his plan was, I let him take it. He lifted my arm and slammed it as hard as he could down onto his raised knee. His intent was to break my arm. And that action did produce a result.

"OW! OW!"

And as I stood there looking down at Red rolling around on the ground and holding onto his bruised knee, I have to admit I felt a little sorry for him.

But I was still smiling.

It was that summer when I launched myself off the high board at the Victoria Pool in a perfect swan dive. Hoping to impress Susie Boyle, the optometrist's blonde daughter on whom I had an unrequited crush. Who didn't even notice either my attempt at scoring a perfect 10 or my incarnadined and somewhat flatter face as I came up after hitting the pool's concrete bottom.

"Man, oh man! You are a mess and you broke off your front tooth," Ralph the lifeguard gasped as I swam to the edge and looked up at him where he was standing at the top of the ladder.

"It's okay," I said with a smile. "At least I didn't lose one of my canine teeth."

"Are you crazy?" was his reply.

And, uh-huh, I just smiled at him through my bloody drool.

I ended up with a temporary cap on that tooth, courtesy of Dr. Bennett, our far from pain-free family dentist. A silver cap, to be precise. Only slightly less visible than a headlight in the middle of my mouth. At the request of the professional photographer who snapped my yearbook picture, my smile was with tight lips.

But the grin on my face during every wrestling match of my senior year exposed that highly artificial addition to my dentition. I grinned so much that when I went to Cornell (with a more natural ivory-colored cap like the one I wear to this day) I was approached by a student who was in my English comp class and had graduated from Linton, one of the schools we wrestled against during that senior year. Back when a news piece in the *Saratogian* referred to me as "Smiling Joe Bruchac, the Western Conference Tournament winner."

My fellow frosh was, it turned out, astounded at the fact that I was one of the two best students in that comp class. (Almost as good as my lifelong friend Peter Klappert, who would go on to win the Yale Younger Poets Award.)

"Man," the Linton guy said, "with that stupid grin of yours we all thought you were a moron."

I suppose it may be because of that smile that there's been more than one time in my life when I've been judged as clueless, naive, or even insincere. And I've heard this remark: "One of these days, Bruchac, you'll learn that there's nothing to smile about."

As if they understood what was behind or beneath that smile. A smile that was an alternative to the tears I shed more than once during that senior year as I continued to mourn the far-too-early death of my grandmother only a few months before. But, even though you might sympathize with some-one deep in loss, there is a point when it just becomes too much. No one person ever invented pain or disappointment or grief all on their own.

Not a smile instead of weeping. But a smile that restores the balance to heart and spirit.

Semi-Buddhist, I suppose. An awareness, perhaps, of the Middle Way. Though I honestly cannot say I knew enough then—or now—about that enlightened path to make any claim of connection. But I do notice how one of my favorite people in the world, His Holiness the Dalai Lama, is always chuckling.

There's an old Haudenosaunee story I have loved since I first heard it long ago. It's the one called "The Boy Who Defeated All His Enemies Through Laughter."

One after another that young man faces terrible creatures trying to kill him. When he goes to a deep spring where a monster lives that has been eating people, that creature rises up and bites off both of the boy's legs. In response the boy just laughs. And as he laughs, his legs grow back. Then, still laughing, he pulls that terrible being out of the water and beats it to death with his club. When he is taken into a sweat lodge by an evil sorcerer who intends to steam him to death, he just laughs and laughs until the sorcerer's head explodes.

It is said by the Haudenosaunee—as my Mohawk elder and friend Tommy Porter explained it to me once—that we human beings have the ability to change our minds. Literally change them, change the way we are thinking. We may find ourselves in what is sometimes called the Twisted Mind. That is when we are thinking and acting selfishly, angrily, or deep in self-pity. Complaining that life is unfair.

But we may choose to think and behave otherwise, to put ourselves into the Good Mind. To realize that life is just life. To return to kindness and generosity, to patience—with others and with yourself. To laughter.

So, as I write this and look into the mirror of my memory, I have to admit that I am still . . .

Smiling Joe.

> On my knees weeding
> catbird floats down from the pine
> to land on my cap

GRAY FOXES

I'm sitting in my cabin up on the backside of Glass Factory Mountain. Years ago, when we first got this place—which is only a mile as the crow flies from Cole Hill where my Abenaki grandfather was born—we converted part of what was a bedroom into a study. Bookshelves line three walls, aside from the desk where I have my computer, which is not connected to either a modem or a cable. No TV up here, no phone. Just me and my writing—and whatever entertainment is available of the nondigital, nonbroadcast kind.

Thinking of which, the fourth wall of my study is taken up by a wide-windowed back door and a window bay from knee height to just below the ceiling. Looking out in the woods that come to within sixty feet of the door.

I'm working on a new novel but see something out of the corner of my left eye as I'm typing. And I hear the catbird whose nest and just-fledged little ones are in the mountain laurels that flank the other side of the cabin. That catbird's mewling call is a warning, quite unlike the multiphonic symphony that issues from its voice box early every morning and every summer day at dusk.

Was it a streak of gray, low to the ground that my mind keeps picturing it after the actual sight has gone?

I hit "save," lift my hands from the keyboard, and slowly swivel my chair. I'm just in time to see a small fox, its tail arced like a question mark, romp by. *Romp* being the appropriate word, not run or lope. It's covering space as if the only purpose of its motion is to express its delight about being alive on a warm summer afternoon like this one.

Was it a gray fox? It had to be. Its fluffy coat was gray along its side, its lower jaw and upper chest a rufous red, black markings on its face, white on its lower chest and belly. As cute and cuddly looking as a stuffed toy. It made me feel like hugging it—with my heart, not my hands. Keeping a respectful distance is one of the best ways we humans can relate to wild things. Being satisfied with just seeing is better than trying to own.

But I'm not seeing it now. It's disappeared. However, it was headed toward the front of the house where the catbird is now verging on hysteria. Which may mean that small fox is still hanging around. I get up, trusting that my motion can't be seen from outside, and walk into the living room to look out the picture window there.

And there it is under one of my pear trees. I can see for sure that it is a gray fox—and not a full-grown one. I know that because, just beyond it, lying next to the blueberry bushes and calmly chowing down on a white-fleshed Anjou pear, holding it firmly between her paws, is a full-grown fox that has to be the first one's mother. Especially obvious by the way that first fox, three-fourths the size of its mom noses up to her, rolls onto its side, and paws at her nose.

She finishes her pear, licks her little one's muzzle. Then she saunters into the woods and the pup follows her. But not far. I can see one ear poking up from the tall royal ferns, the green stems trembling as it moves among them.

Patience is one of the best things to cultivate if you really want to see things. That's one thing my grampa taught me, though his exact words were more like "Just set still." Which I do as I go back to my chair. And within a matter of minutes my patience pays, with dividends. Her afternoon snack complete, the mother fox trots up in the middle of the small, dry, more-or-less lawn (more or less because I neither seed nor water it) just outside my study, flattens out on the ground and rolls onto her back, then onto her stomach. She seems both relaxed and alert as she starts to groom herself like a cat, her ears always cocked for any threat.

She's soon joined by that first cub—or maybe not. Its tail looks thinner, the tip blacker. Then "maybe not" becomes "for sure" as the original cub leaps out of the yellow-blossomed ligularias, drops down into the "let's play" posture known to every member of the dog family, and the two cubs begin chasing each other in circles around the planter where the cherry tomatoes are still in yellow blossom. Leaping, turning in midair to pounce on each other, those two little foxes are better than a nature documentary.

It's been said by behavioral scientists that the intelligence of an animal relates to play behavior. Playing builds their muscles, sharpens their coordination, readies them for their role as near-apex predators. The smarter they are, the more they play. By which measure, my backyard visitors may rank as a bunch of furry little Einsteins. And also, I realize when I think about it, the reason why the chipmunk and squirrel population around my cabin, so large a mere month ago, has been markedly less evident of late.

I watch the three gray foxes interact like that for another half an hour, thinking it can't get any better than this—even

though the catbird flitting in and out to perch discontent-
edly just outside the window clearly disagrees. But I'm wrong
again. A third cub suddenly bursts from beneath the rhodo-
dendrons and joins them.

More than an hour has passed and the show is still
going on, punctuated by furry exits and curtain calls. My
whole backyard and the nearby woods has transformed into
a vulpine playground. Everything is Zen to them, pure begin-
ner's mind. A single purple petal plucked from a flowering
hosta becomes a game as the first cub tosses it up into the air,
watches it flutter, chases it, catches it, tosses it again. The sticks
I've placed to mark where pink lady's slippers grow are perfect
to chew. The ramp leading up to my storage shed is an excellent surface to wrestle upon and roll down.

I've put away my novel; opened up a new file to write
this. It's now five o'clock in the afternoon and I suppose I need
to think about other things that need to be done—including
that grocery shopping if I want to eat today. But who needs
food when you have what I've had for the last two hours?

Still, there's been no sign of any of them for a full ten
minutes since the mother fox laid her ears back, got low to the
ground, and vanished behind the big pines. The show may be
over, folks.

But wait. There at the edge of the woods, as if she
materialized out of the air, is the mother fox. She's nosing
something I can barely see aside from its white belly. Then,

with the greatest delicacy, she picks it up in her jaws. A rabbit she's just caught. Trots off into the woods with its limp body toward those three young ones who are about to eat. I may have been ignoring my own need for food, but not her and her cubs.

Play with your whole being, but don't forget to care for your family.

There's no need to work any further on my novel today. I've been given lessons enough to think about and to share. Thanks to the gray foxes.

Asparagus shoots
pushing up through the brown leaves
our first green harvest

MSKIKOIKAS

MOON OF STRAWBERRIES

STRAWBERRIES

That's what the hand-lettered sign on the corner of Daniels Road read, reminding me that once again it's the season our Old People call the Strawberry Moon.

There are stories about how the strawberry came to be, and one of my favorite ones come from Haudenosaunee (Iroquois) tradition. I think I heard it first from Tehanetorens/ Ray Fadden. I was seven years old then, and he was working with his family at a tourist attraction just outside Lake George, New York, called Indian Village.

There was an orphan boy. He was hunting down by the river when he heard small voices coming from somewhere. He looked down. There, near his feet, were two tiny men with bows and arrows. They were trying to shoot a black squirrel at the top of an oak tree, but their arrows could not reach it.

That boy was a good hunter, which meant that he hunted for others more than for himself. So, he decided to help those little men. He shot that squirrel, and when it fell to the ground he told the tiny men that it was theirs. They were so happy, they invited him to come to their village. The boy followed them as they carried that squirrel down to the river where they loaded it into their little canoe.

"Now get in," they told him.

He took one step and as soon as he did, he shrank down to the same size as the little men and was in that canoe. His new friends dipped their paddles into the water. Once they did so, that canoe lifted up and began to fly through the air. It flew straight toward a cliff. Just before it hit, the cliff opened up, and they passed through it and landed in a village. Everyone in the village welcomed that boy.

They gave him a special drink he had never had before, one that was sweet to the taste. It was made from a fruit he had never seen that they told him was called a strawberry. He stayed with the villagers for a few days, and when he left to go back to his home they gave him one big strawberry—almost as big as he was.

"Here," they said. "This is a gift for you and your people."

He climbed to the top of the hill. There on the other side was his village. He was so surprised that he dropped the strawberry he'd been carrying. As soon as it touched the ground, it shrank down until it was very small. Then, where it fell, vines began to grow everywhere with beautiful red strawberries on them glowing as bright as coals from a fire.

Somehow, his village looked different. When he entered it people came up to him.

"Who are you?" they asked.

"Don't you know me? he replied. "I am the little orphan boy of your village."

"How could you say that? You are not a boy. You are a tall man."

He looked at himself and realized he was no longer a little boy. Years had passed while he was in the village of the little people.

He took the people to the field where those strawberries were growing. He showed them how to pick those berries and make that special drink the little people had given him. From then on, every year, the strawberries returned.

And, ever since then, to give thanks to those little people for that gift, a special ceremony has been done. As they dance, a certain song is sung in the darkness of the lodge at night. If it is done correctly, the people will hear the little people's voices join theirs and they will all dance together giving thanks for the sweet gift of strawberries.

To this day, strawberries—the first fruit of the new year—are very special to all the People of the Longhouse. When my dear friend, the late poet Maurice Kenny, founded his small press he named it Strawberry Press, in honor of that fruit and his own Iroquois ancestry.

Maurice also reminded me, more than once, that when you leave this life, you travel up the Milky Way to a place in the stars where the strawberries are always ripe. Every time Maurice was sick—and during the many years I knew him he suffered several life-threatening illnesses—he would say to me, "Joe, I almost tasted strawberries."

One of my favorite poems of Maurice's is about being given some strawberries out of season—berries from Mexico. Their taste is woody and not at all pleasant—a metaphor for a number of things, including the mistreatment of immigrants, the near-slave labor on farms in other southern nations that provide us with fruit out of season. Maurice never shied away from making political or controversial statements.

I enjoy the sweet taste of fresh berries grown locally, but that taste is nothing like that of wild strawberries. Even though they are small, smaller than your fingernail, their taste is special.

My mother loved those wild berries, as well as other natural foods, gifts from the natural world around us.

"Would you go and get me some marsh marigolds? I saw them flowering down in the swamp today," she would say.

Or, "Can you go cut me some dandelions. I'd love to cook up some of those greens."

But she never asked me to pick wild strawberries for her. That was something she had to do all by herself. I only have to close my eyes to see her sitting in the upper field, a basket by her side. Even when her knees were so bad that she could barely walk, she would still make her slow, painful way up there each June when that sweet gift returned.

There is a different story about how strawberries came to the people told by the Cherokees. I heard several versions of that story told over the years. It became one that I knew so well that when a new friend of mine asked if I had any stories about plants—since she was an illustrator and liked to draw them—my first thought was about that story.

That new friend, Anna Vojtech, had been introduced to me by the wonderful storyteller Judith Black. Judith thought we had a lot in common. My own ancestry on my father's side is Slovak and Anna was from what was then still Czechoslovakia.

So I wrote down for Anna the story of how strawberries came to be. It was close to the version I learned from Jean Starr, a Cherokee friend from Oklahoma.

Anna thanked me and then, over the course of the next few months, sent me some pictures she had drawn illustrating that story. I loved her illustrations—she's a superb artist—and told her that.

It's a simple tale but a very deep one. Back when first human beings came to be, First Man and First Woman had an argument about something. Whatever it was, First Man did not behave well. So First Woman said, "I'm not going to live with you any longer," and walked out.

First Man was immediately sorry. He tried to catch her to apologize, but she was too fast for him. That is when he did the first smart thing he'd done that day. He looked up into the sky at the Sun and asked the Sun for help.

Sun agreed. She shone down in front of First Woman, and where Sun's light touched the ground raspberries grew. First Woman paid no attention to them. Sun shone a second time. Blueberry bushes shot up. First Woman walked right past them.

Sun saw she would have to try harder. So this time her light made blackberries grow—tall canes loaded with luscious fruit. First Woman did not stop for them either.

Finally, Sun did her best, shining down with the kind of warmth you find in love and sharing. And this time small green plants spread all over the ground, covered with little red berries, each in the shape of a heart.

First Woman could go no farther without stepping on them. She noticed the sweet smell coming from those berries, bent down, picked one, and tasted it. Their taste was so good that she decided to pick some to share with her husband.

She was still picking them when he finally caught up to her. He apologized and then they shared those berries. That was how the strawberries came to be, and each year they are the first fruit to ripen.

I'd thought those drawings Anna sent me were the end of it. But then, perhaps a year later, I got a phone call.

"Joseph," a voice said. "I have great news. Our book is going to be published."

"Who is this?" I asked.

"It is Anna," she replied. "And our book is going to be published by Dial."

"What book?"

"*The First Strawberries*."

What I had not realized was that Anna had been sending the manuscript of my story and her illustrations out to publishers. So, I ended up getting a book published without ever submitting it.

Ironically, not long after that unexpected news from Anna I received a letter in the mail from a different well-known publisher of children's books. In that envelope was a rejection slip that read something along the lines of: "We are sorry, but we are unable to publish your manuscript."

I immediately wrote back to them.

"I am sorry," I said, "but I cannot accept your rejection because I have never submitted anything to your press."

My rejection of their rejection was followed shortly thereafter by a very apologetic letter from the publisher. Somehow my name and address—on a list of writers they wished to solicit work from—had ended up on another list—a list of the people who had already submitted work and were being rejected.

The First Strawberries remains in print, and I am happy that it was published. But I always like to remind people that that brief telling is not the full story. For example, it does not mention that the Sun, who decides to help First Man, is a woman.

My dear friend Gayle Ross, who is truly one of the best storytellers in the world and draws her own tellings from her Cherokee ancestry, sees that story as a reminder of the power of all women. Among the Aniyunwiya—as among the Haudenosaunee—the women have great power and a central place in their nation. As Gayle once said to me (though these are not her exact words), among her people the women owned the homes, the fields, and were the heads of the family. All that the men owned were their clothing and their weapons.

"It was pretty much a perfect society," Gayle added.

So it is that today, in the heart of that Moon of Strawberries, I find myself grateful not just for the taste of that first fruit but for the gifts and the guidance of all the women in my life, especially our Mother Earth from whom all such blessings flow.

Ripe red strawberries
gift of the Little People
so good to see you

DREAMS

It was just a dream.

Let me make sure that's clear before I start. What I had, just before waking up this fine June morning, was just a dream, okay?

The red car spinning out of control like a carnival ride come loose from its moorings despite the fact that I'm turning into the skid. Then whomp, hitting hard into the high snowbank at the edge of the hill. An avalanche cascading down to bury the car and me.

A dream, yeah. But also an echo, a reflection, a replay of "Been there, done that."

And, somehow, there I am standing in the road and watching as the county crews dig out one car after another, all of them buried in that cataclysmic slide. A black Bronco, a green Chevy truck, a silver VW, an old Blue Plymouth, and then a newer gold one with those high 1960 fish fins.

Okay, fine. I get it. Very interesting, this opening memory vault of my cerebral cortex. All cars that I used to own.

One vehicle after another. But where the heck is my Nissan? My wallet is in that car and my coat and I'm standing here in the cold barefooted. I can't even remember my license number. And was I actually in the Nissan? Or was I driving the Honda SRV?

By the way, I am now awake. And fully aware that all of this was just a dream, even though my eyes are still shut. However, dang it, I can't leave it like this. I need to go back to sleep, need to will myself back into that dream to get my car.

Does all that sound a little familiar? Anything like that ever happen to you? Knowing that it was not really "real," but wanting desperately to get back into that wrong unreality to right it or maybe rewrite it?

Dreams. Don't get me wrong. They are not something I would make light of—those visitors that sometimes come to us out of that darkness made visible. Our Old People—no matter what land or nation they came from—took dreams seriously. Still do. Here in the Northeast, when the Jesuit missionaries were proselytizing among our Native nations (and doing a bit of spying for France on the side) they were astounded at the role dreams played among, for example, the Wendat (or Wyandot), the people they called Hurons. In *The Jesuit Relations*, the letters sent back to France by those missionaries, Father Brebeauf wrote this in 1636 about the Huron view of dreams:

They have a faith in dreams which surpasses all belief; and if Christians were to put into execution all their divine inspirations with as much care as our Savages carry out their dreams, no doubt they would very soon become great Saints. They look upon their dreams as ordinances and irrevocable decrees, the execution of which it is not permitted without crime to delay. . . .

The dream is the oracle that all these poor Peoples consult and listen to, the Prophet which predicts to them future events. . . .

They hold nothing so precious that they would not readily deprive themselves of it for the sake of a dream. If they have been successful in hunting, if they bring back their Canoes laden with fish, all this is at the discretion of a dream; . .

It prescribes their feasts, their dances, their songs, their games,—in a word, the dream does everything.

It's 1992. This is not a dream. My son Jesse and I have just come out of the Yucatan rain forest. Before us is the small Lacandon Mayan village of Naha. The sudden tropic darkness has closed in, the sounds of the night's creatures are all around us. We walk toward the lighted doorway of the largest building in the village. No bigger than an elongated garage, its walls are made of sticks, its roof is thatch.

We look inside. There by the fire sits Old Chan Kin, Chan Kin Viejo, in a white cotton tunic, just like the ones that all the people of his village wear. Around him are all the others, from the youngest to the oldest, sitting at his feet as he speaks the story that will fill their hearts.

"*Nla ketch,*" he says, beckoning us inside with the ancient Lacandon greeting that roughly means "I am another yourself."

My son Jesse and I are escorted by Robert Bruce, the American anthropologist who spent most of his adult life not just studying but also advocating for the Lacandon people. And so, because he speaks their language and because of their tradition of open friendship toward visitors, we settle in easily to life in Naha—which is both the name of the village and the nearby lake and means "The Water House."

The time spent in Naha, though only a few days, is something I could write about at great length. There was so much to learn from the people's long, sustained, and sustainable relationship with the rain forest; from Chan Kin himself, whose name might be rendered in English as "Little Sun" or "Little Prophet." At that time he was, by Robert's reckoning, more than 120 years old and as vigorous as someone many decades younger.

Every day, first thing after we woke, Chan Kin would ask us of our dreams and then interpret them. For every dream, he explained, holds a meaning, may suggest a path to follow or predict the future.

One morning when he asked what I dreamt, this is what I said.

"I dreamt that I had a small dog and that I sold it."

Chan Kin's face became very serious. He paused before he spoke rapidly in Lacandon to Robert, who nodded.

"Joe," Robert said, "Chan Kin said that a dream such as that can be taken to mean that a serious illness is coming to you."

Then Chan Kin laughed. "On the other hand," he said, "it may just mean that you are going to sell your little dog."

Each morning, after telling our dreams, we'd walk down to wash by the water tank that overflowed from a spring. Aside from brushing them away, I did not take much note of the gnats that flew up and bit my legs every time we went there.

But then, when I got back home, I noticed that one of those gnat bites was not healing. In fact, it was getting redder and the skin was becoming necrotic. I visited one doctor after another and got varying opinions, like I might have been bitten by a spider such as a brown recluse. Weeks passed and then months. I now had a hole in my left ankle about down to the bone—and satellite eruptions on both legs in various places.

None of the doctors I visited knew much about tropical parasites—of which I, alas, already knew more than I wished. The three years I'd spent in the late 1960s as a volunteer teacher in Ghana, West Africa, had resulted (among other things, no mention of amoebic dysentery, please!) in my body being adopted as a permanent franchise for those unicellular organisms of the genus Plasmodium—known commonly as malaria.

Despite their lack of success in curing my worsening condition, my physicians delighted in examining this new phenomenon and recording their failed attempts at treatment.

"I'm going to do a paper on this," one enthusiastic skin specialist said.

Another, while studying and photographing it said, "Oh, this looks much better."

"My wound looks better?" I said.

"No," he replied, "this picture I took is much better than the last one."

What I had was cutaneous leishmaniasis, a protozoan parasite transmitted by a bite from an infected female sand fly. Common enough in tropical areas and a close cousin to "Baghdad boil," as the similar skin ailment would be called by American troops dispatched to Iraq first in the Gulf War of 1990–1991 and then in the much higher-budget sequel a little over a decade later.

Today you can Google it. Leishmaniasis. You'll find not only a graphic description—with photos—of what I suffered from, you also can find the cure for it. Which none of my doctors could do a global search for, seeing as how Google was still in the future as of 1992.

Luckily, after a year of getting used to having a permanently open, gruesomely oozing abscess on my ankle (not fun kids, do not try this at home), I mentioned it to David Richmond, a Mohawk friend of mine.

"Why don't you try a potato poultice?" he said, looking at it. "That's what my aunt would do."

So I did. Grated a potato, applied the gratings to the wound. Watched as said gratings turned blue, then black, drying in and over the crater in my skin. Kept that up for a week. And then another. Until, a dozen or so potatoes later, the dang thing was healed.

I would find out, a few months after that, in a phone conversation with Robert Bruce, that he had also experienced leishmaniasis.

"Always seems to hit your ankles," he said. "The Mayans, though, they know just how to get rid of it. They do it with a potato poultice."

But what does this have to do with that dream of mine in 1992 about selling a small dog?

First, just as Chan Kin said, that dream of mine presaged (if not predicted) a serious illness.

Second (coincidentally, of course, eh?), when that wound finally did heal it left behind a brown scar on my skin in the shape (still there thirty years later) of a small dog.

So, as I look at that scar and consider that car crash dream I just had, I'll be driving very carefully today, even though what I had last night was . . . just a dream.

Clouds of pollen flow
from the top of the white pine
early morning light

LIBRARIES

Last night I dreamed I was walking into a library on some college campus. It was an old stone building, and the big room I entered was filled with students sitting in comfortable chairs and reading.

It was one of those dreams where I was aware that I was dreaming. The giveaway that it had to be a dream was that all those young people I saw in that dream were reading books, not texting or playing games on their iPads. For sure not present-day reality.

So, when I woke—the sound of the catbird greeting the early summer day outside my window—it was with the memory of that library in my mind and a smile on my face. I was amused that my subconscious had set such a nostalgic scene for me as I wandered through that big room, pulling down from the shelves and happily perusing leather-bound volumes that would have been locked away in a temperature-controlled rare book vault in an actual academic setting.

It was, to say the least, a good dream.

Other men dream of beautiful women and tropical beaches, of being sports heroes and movie stars, and your vision of paradise is a flipping library? Not the pleasure dome of Kubla Khan? Bruchac, what is wrong with you?

That dream, of course, might simply have floated up from the deep, roiled waters of my cerebral cortex because of recent events. Two transactions in particular. One being the month or more I spent putting together the latest installment of my archive. Twenty boxes of my manuscripts, early drafts, bound galleys and the like loaded into his van yesterday by my good friend Ken Lopez to be bundled off to the Beinecke Library in Yale.

The other was the visit two days ago of the daughter of a dear, much respected friend who is dying of cancer and wanted to donate to me all the American Indian books she'd accumulated over the years. Seven boxes so big they weighed down the springs in her daughter's car, and I had to use a hand cart to move them into my garage.

I haven't yet opened those boxes, lifted those books out, opened each of them knowing that Susan's eyes will never look at those pages again. That her generous heart will no longer be beating when I place the last of those last gifts of hers on the upstairs shelves in our reading area next to the dorm rooms of our Ndakinna Education Center.

The other source of my library dream might have been a residual memory of the moment last week when I moused my screen's arrow onto the Friend icon for Stephen Motika. Stephen is a gifted and energetic young poet and a staff member at Poets House in New York City. That one click brought to mind—well, in virtual actuality, transported me to—Poets House itself. That gorgeous building on the banks of the Hudson River. With its immense, friendly, accessible library of books of poetry (including a few hundred I've donated), the readings and writing workshops that take place there, the aura of immanent creativity that throbs about its environs. A few years ago, I was lucky enough to be part of a gathering there of younger and older American Indian poets. And over the years I've donated hundreds of books to Poets House—such as my entire collection of student anthologies from poetry in the school workshops I taught in the 1970s and 1980s, as well as obscure volumes of poetry from other countries collected over the years.

But, to be honest, I probably didn't need any sort of recent key for that dream to open the door of my mind and visit me. Libraries are often in my thoughts and my dreams. They've been so ever since I learned to read and discovered as a young child that there were actually places where I could not just look at but also borrow books.

I can take them home with me?

For free?

Holy Moly! Are you kidding?

Saratoga Springs has a wonderful public library in a new building that opened in 1995. (Saratoga is a city that enthusiastically supports its library. Its voters easily pass the library budget every year.) My son Jesse and I were in that library just last Monday, doing a Native music and storytelling program in the Harry Dutcher Community Room.

The old public library, a block away, is now the home of our local arts council, Saratoga Arts. Its basement once held the Children's Room. I was seven when it opened.

"Come with me, Sonny," my grandmother said. "I've got something just wonderful to show you."

She didn't tell me what it was, just had me climb into the old blue Plymouth leaving my grandfather to watch the store. We drove the interminable three miles to town. Parked in front of the big old decaying Grand Union Hotel. Walked across Broadway to the Public Library. But we didn't go in the front door. We continued down around the back to the entrance from Congress Park.

And entered another world. Paradise. Valhalla. Eden. Carcassonne. Elysium. Arcadia.

My grandmother was saying something to me, introducing me to a smiling middle-aged woman who was shaking my hand.

"This is the new Children's Room of our library," the woman said. "All of the books in here are for young people just like you."

I stood there, stunned into silence. Every wall was covered with books, colorful spines rainbowing the shelves. To my entranced eyes they glowed brighter than the jewels I'd imagined in Ali Baba's Arabian Nights cave. For a moment I forgot how to breathe.

Finally, I managed to force speech out of my mouth, taking a breath between each word.

"I . . . am . . . going . . . to . . . read . . . every . . . book . . . in . . . here."

Although it took me seven years, I nearly managed to do that. I probably would have succeeded had the library not kept adding new titles.

That night at home in my little downstairs bedroom, the door open to the next room where my grandparents lay, I didn't stay awake as I usually did. I only called out (like always), "Good Night, Sweet Dreams, I Love You" one time. Not half a dozen times, desperate to be reassured by their patient response with those same magic words that my two precious Old People were still alive and breathing.

No, that night after my first visit to the Children's Room of the Saratoga Public Library, I went right to sleep. And my dreams of wandering among shelves, filled with the infinite possibilities of all those pages, were sweet.

Like every dream I've ever had of libraries.

Cooper's hawk swoops low
as the mourning doves scatter
Look out, red squirrel

THE BLANKET TREE

It's early summer, near the end of the Strawberry Moon. I'm in the woods about to peel bark from the *maskwamoziak* as we call them in Abenaki—the blanket trees. Birch is their Igliz-moniwi (English) name.

Maskwamozi. Blanket tree. The one whose skin covered our lodges. I love the way the Abenaki words that first spoke themselves to the minds of my elders countless centuries ago, so often catch the sense and the spirit of the beings with whom we share this circle of existence. Know the true name and we may know the use, know what to be thankful for. Or, at the very least, better understand and respect.

> There's a story we tell
> of *maskwamozi.*
>
> Once a little girl
> was out with her parents
> walking through the forest.
>
> Her parents were quarreling
> with each other
> and did not notice
> their daughter
> had fallen behind.

When they reached their wigwam,
they turned around
to look for her
but she was gone.

It was growing dark
and then the snow
began to fall
as they looked for her.

All through the night
they searched for her,
calling her name,
fearing that she
had frozen
in the sudden cold.

But with the morning light
they found their daughter,
alive and warm,
asleep beneath
an old birch tree,
a roll of its bark
wrapped around her.

As I stand carefully surveying the birch trees, I feel a sort of completeness here in the forest. It's a connection harder to make when I'm inside. Part of me longs to just stay here in the woods all day. Not just step briefly into the forest but instead remain outside the boundaries of clock time and the restrictions of responsibility to anything other than the ancient cycles of each season.

Interruption for a disclaimer in the interest of honesty. I am not surrendering to a fantasy of dwelling at one with all the happy little forest creatures. There are deer ticks and mosquitoes here. Also it is soon going to be horsefly season. Some part of nature is always willing and able to eat us.

I think back on my three years of volunteer teaching in the West African nation of Ghana. They were a reality check against my childhood longing, seduced by the admittedly racist novels of Edgar Rice Burroughs, to live as did Tarzan in the rain forest, swinging blithely, an overly muscled exemplar of the "master race," on conveniently hung vines from tree to tree. When I first set foot in a real rain forest, just off the road to Kumasi, I saw a hanging vine perfect for swinging on. I grabbed it—and the result was a cascade of fiercely biting red ants falling from that vine and on down my back and my neck. The long ululating yell I let out then was much like that of the legendary ape man.

In truth, only a part of me wants that forest fantasy. Another sizable portion is perfectly content ensconced in a comfortable chair with a pint of strawberry ice cream and reading. Or sitting as I am right now at my keyboard.

There is no such thing as an easy life.

But, having said that, there is also such a thing as trying to live that life in a good way. And for me that involves spending time as often as possible out in *ktsi kpiwi*, the big woods my grandfather first introduced me to when I was two years old. Which brings me back to birch trees.

I run my palms along the smooth body of the first tree that drew me to it, its pale, straight trunk is such a contrast among the brown maples and even darker pines. Its color is not the pure, untouched whiteness of new snow. It's a page marked by a black script written in a language that speaks of seasons and decades. An ancient language, it's one that speaks to those of us fortunate enough to have heard and remembered what elders shared.

On the trunk of the birch, upside-down Vs show where branches once grew. Those marks resemble outstretched wings, the sign of the Thunder Beings. Our Anishinabe cousins to the west see the thunders as immense birds with wings that spread from horizon to horizon, lightning flashing from their eyes. We Wabanaki know them as the Bedagiak, grandfathers who ride the dark clouds, hurling down arrows of lightning to cleanse the land of evil. They love the birch, and those marks are proof of that love.

I've been told (though white meteorologists view such Native folk traditions as bunk) that birch is the safest tree to shelter beneath during a thunderstorm. The Bedagiak seldom choose to strike it with their arrows. As if in proof of that, there's a lightning scar down the trunk of a big maple only twenty yards away from me, a tree shorter than this tall birch.

I look farther up the trunk of the birch. There's an ascending series of scratches, sets of four parallel lines incised into the tree, leaving little curlicues of bark as thin as tissue paper. Claw marks from the animal that climbed it. Not big enough or deep enough to be the sign of a young bear scrambling up. Most likely the porcupine I greeted near here a few days ago. If you know what to look for, you can read a lot in the woods.

I reach into my pocket to take out my tobacco pouch. Always make a physical expression of your gratitude. At least that is how I was taught. Tobacco is a sacred gift. It is only when misused that it becomes a harmful addiction. It was given to us to be shared with all Creation, to be offered as a sign of thanks, burned to carry our prayers up to Ktsi Nwaskw, the Great Mystery with its smoke.

> We didn't always have tobacco.
> Once all the tobacco
> in the world was owned
> by a terrible being known as Cols.

A giant creature
who flew through the air,
the sound of his wings
was louder than thunder.

Cols kept that tobacco
and shared it with no one.
He used its power selfishly.

Gluskonba,
the one who made
himself from words,
knew this was wrong.

He went to the island
where Cols lived.
All around that island
were the bleached bones
of people who'd come
to get tobacco.

Cols came flying
down at Gluskonba
the sound of his wings
like rattling bones.

But Gluskonba
grabbed hold of Cols.
Stroking him from head to toe,
he made Cols smaller
and smaller and smaller
until he was only
a grasshopper.

Then Gluskonba put just a little
of that tobacco into the tiny mouth
of Cols, so he always
would have some of that sacred gift.

But the rest of that tobacco
was given to the Alnobak,
the human beings.

To this day, Cols will sometimes
fly up and surprise you
with the rattling of his wings,
but he is no longer a danger.

So it is today
that tobacco is in
the hands of the people—
who must always remember
to share it and use it for prayer.

I know from my own experience that it's always a good thing to give tobacco when you are taking something from the natural world. If nothing else, offering tobacco makes you pause, makes you mindful.

I remember a time two decades ago near Fairbanks, Alaska. I'd given a talk at the university there and had been invited to a reception at the home of my friend Jim Ruppert. In his backyard was a pile of birch logs cut for firewood. Jim gave me permission to peel some of that bark—as long as I didn't take too long since the guests would soon be arriving. I was in such a hurry to peel that bark that I didn't bother to make an offering or even express my thanks verbally. As I made the first cut, the knife slipped in my hand and sliced into my palm. I ended up offering not tobacco, but some of my blood to the Alaskan earth in exchange for that bark.

I take tobacco from my pouch. It's not commercially grown but *Nicotiana rustica*, the old Indian tobacco we call *wdamo wabanaki*. I raised it from seeds passed on to me by Tom Porter, a Mohawk elder whose Indian name Sakokwenionkwas means "One Who Wins." Tom is a man known to those fortunate enough to be in his presence as one of the most generous of teachers. And because it is important to always remember our teachers, it's with his gentle face in my mind that I carefully place the tobacco at the base of the birch.

Wliwini, nidoba maskwamozi
Thanks, friend blanket tree
Ktsi wliwini odzi kia
Great thanks to you

Then I make the first long cut from top to bottom. I press the knife into the trunk just deep enough to take off that top layer. When you girdle most trees, slicing through the outer layer of growth, you sever the phloem, that complex vascular tissue of sieve tubes and companion cells where nutrients are carried up from the roots. Strip the bark all the way around an ash, an elm, a basswood—and it will die.

But not the blanket tree. Birch can shed its outer layer without great harm to the tree. If you walk through the forests near many of our contemporary Native communities where there are birch trees, you'll see tree after tree whose bark has been respectfully harvested, wide rings of light brown wood showing where birches gave up their blankets.

All along the trail
I see the marks
of people who came
to these hills before me,
there in the remembering trees

People who work the woods can tell you that every tree gives off its own odor when you cut into it. Your hands and clothes and hair take on that smell. When you come home at night, you are bringing the breath of the forest with you. I remember how my grandfather smelled after a day of working in the pine woods. Moist sawdust stuck on his boots, his hands—which were already brown as earth—even darker from the sap of the trees, the woods scent all around him.

Pine is sharp and tangy. Beech is like peppermint. And the scent released from birch is a bit like that of beech, but not as strong. It's a clean, refreshing smell, as subtle an odor as the earth-making aroma of the cushioning layer of old leaves and pine needles beneath my bare feet.

I finish the vertical cut and follow it with two more around the tree. One at the top, one at the bottom, going from left to right. That's the direction in which to peel the bark. I know no other reason for this than that I was told to do it that way. Everywhere I've been where birch bark is peeled by Native people—Athabascans in Alaska, Anishinabes in Wisconsin, Penobscots in Maine—I've heard that's the right way to do it.

It makes as much sense as what I was told by a certain medicine person about the way to gather the bark from another plant I'm not going to name. Peel it upward and you can use it as an emetic. Peel it downward and it becomes a diuretic. Not exactly logical in the Western way of thinking. But who cares as long as it works?

The piece of bark I'm about to peel will be a shingle about three feet by three feet. No particular reason for that size other than we can manage it easily and there are no large knots or rough places in the bark within that expanse that would make peeling harder. It is plenty big enough to be a nice-sized section of the covering we'll use to clothe the wigwam at our Ndakinna Education Center—the ninety-acre family forest preserve my mom put into a conservation easement twenty years ago where my sons and I teach.

I loosen the bark with the edge of my hatchet, begin to work my fingers up and down. And the bark starts to loosen. I go slow, applying steady, careful pressure as it makes little tearing noises, almost like Velcro letting go. Then, with a popping sound, the big piece of bark releases itself from the layer of growth beneath, leaping off the tree into my hands. A gift to be accepted and used with care, a good start for this day of peeling birch bark.

Peeling bark
my hands are touching
all those who touched
this tree before me

Two-legged and
four-legged ones
and those who fly

With a sharpened twig
I draw their shapes
on the brown inner bark

so doing, I know
their spirits will come
will speak to me
in my dreams

PAD8GIKAS

MOON OF THUNDER

SQUIRRELS

I look out the kitchen window at the bird feeders. Even though it's July, a time when some people bring in their feeders, we keep ours out year-round.

Yesterday morning at this time they were thronging with chickadees, nuthatches, goldfinches in their gold summer plumage, slate-colored juncos. Swooping in to perch briefly, peck down and then dart back to the flowering Rose of Sharon bushes thirty feet away.

Got my sunflower seed. Your turn now.

One after another like tiny members of a feathered tag team.

But there are no birds on the feeders right now, though I can see several black-capped chickadees in the low limbs of the hemlock beyond my garden pond.

The reason for the absence of any avian diners is squatting in the one feeder that is still half full. Its brushy tail arched over its back, a red squirrel is stuffing seeds into its mouth with both paws. As single-mindedly determined as a contestant in a hot-dog eating contest.

It is a beautiful little creature if you look at it closely. The one dark eye turned in my direction is ringed with white. A black stripe along its side separates its white underside from its reddish-brown back. And it is perfectly designed for the life it leads. The muscles that ripple under its skin enable it to take great leaps. Its dexterous, clawed feet have a grip strength that is off the charts in human terms, and it can scale almost any wall, even the slick shingles on the side of a house.

I tap once lightly on the window. The red squirrel hurls itself off the feeder, leaving it swinging wildly as it bounds to the nearest of the big pines. As soon as it is gone flights of chickadees begin returning. But I know that squirrel or one of its larger gray cousins will soon be back at my feeders, especially after I've refilled them later today.

C'est la vie. C'est la guerre. C'est la Tamiasciurus hudsonicus *et* Sciurus carolinensis.

I don't let squirrels drive me nuts like some people do. I'll just refill the feeders more often and let go of that desire to control everything beyond my control. It's amazing how crazy people can get when nature takes its course in front of their eyes.

Such as the time when I was sitting by a pond on the campus of the University of Florida in Gainesville, watching a mother duck and four fluffy little golden ducklings drifting across the lambent surface. It was a place I'd been before, so I was not unprepared for what happened next. But the nearby lanky young college guy in a Gators T-shirt walking hand in hand with his girlfriend was not.

Just as he was saying "Aw, look at those cute little duckli . . ."

SNAP! The jaws of the small alligator that lived in that pond closed on the rearmost member of the small flock and, as the survivors flapped and squawked toward shore, dragged it down leaving only a swirl in its wake.

"That gator just grabbed that duckling!" the college guy screamed. An accurate, albeit hysterical observation.

Then his girlfriend fell to her knees sobbing.

"No, no, no!" he screamed.

He began picking up stones and hurling them into the pond. Then, no more stones in sight, he grabbed a nearby stick and waded in.

"Let it go!" he shouted, striking the surface. "Let it go, let it go!"

That was exactly the suggestion I thought of making to that young man at that moment. However, my better judgment overruled my doing anything other than tiptoeing away while he, like the Irish hero Cuchulain fighting the waves of the sea, kept flailing madly at the unresponsive water.

Getting back to squirrels, you might not believe the various lengths that avid bird fanciers go to try to keep squirrels away from those seeds that have been put out *only* for our feathered friends. You can find videos on the internet of acrobat squirrels running gauntlets of wires, cone-shaped baffles, greased poles, and everything short of electrified fences to get to those black oil sunflower that are the rodent equivalent of crack. It's fun to watch them, and if squirrels were not so common—even in our cities—I could imagine folks being delighted by the sight of them.

Not that squirrels, fluffy and chubby and cute as they may appear to be, are actually all that cuddly. In addition to purloined sunflower seeds, the diet of both the red and gray squirrel might be described as not just omnivorous but voracious. In addition to pine cones and the nuts of various trees, squirrels enjoy varying their diet with not only birds' eggs, but also nestlings. And those chisel teeth can take a bite out of your flesh as well.

One of our old Abenaki stories tells how Gluskonba called the animals together for a council, a story I've already mentioned in an earlier essay. It was because the weakest ones in Creation, the human beings would soon arrive. Gluskonba was worried how the animals would react to them, especially because many of the four-legged ones back then were so much larger and more powerful than the creatures of today. When he asked each animal how it would react to its first sight of a human, Ktsi Awasos, Great Bear, said it would swallow that new being with one gulp. Ktsi Moz, Great Moose, said it would spear every human with its horns and trample it. So Gluskonba changed each of those animals, made them smaller and less dangerous.

Then he came to the giant creature all the others feared, the one called Ktsi Mikwe in Abenaki. Of all the four-leggeds, it was the most vicious, dangerous, and bad tempered.

"What will you do when you see human beings?" Gluskonba asked.

"I will crush them with big stones, I will tear them apart with my teeth and claws, I will destroy every human being in the world," Ktsi Mikwe snarled.

So, when Gluskonba changed Ktsi Mikwe, he made him very small, so small that he fit into the palm of Gluskonba's hand. Then Mikwe leaped from his hand and ran to the tops of the trees. That is where Mikwe, or Red Squirrel, still can be found to this day. And, though small, he still has a bad temper. Often, when you walk through the forest, Red Squirrel will hurl down twigs, pine cones, and acorns, trying to crush you as he screams, "I will destroy you!"

Gray squirrels, by the way, are said to be afraid of red squirrels. My father explained that was because, even though they are smaller, red squirrels are tougher and quicker.

"They chase a gray squirrel," Dad said, "they always attack it from behind, trying to castrate it. That's why you never see gray squirrels living anywhere near red squirrels."

I used to think all of that might just be a folk belief. After all, I've observed plenty of places where red squirrels and gray squirrels operated in close proximity. Especially when it came to my bird feeders. Then, just yesterday, I watched a determined red squirrel chase a very large gray fifty yards down Ridge Road, darting in several times to nip at its hindquarters under its tail. Hoo-ha!

I have never seen a gray squirrel venture onto one of our feeders when a red squirrel is there.

Speaking of which, both of my bird feeders are empty now, aside from two or three chickadees whose demeanor might be described as either expectant or resentful—depending on how much anthropomorphism you wish to overlay the other inhabitants of the natural world with. Even the little square cages in which I place suet are as empty as any attempts I might make to limit my largesse to those of the feathery persuasion.

Time to put out more food for the birds . . . and the squirrels.

Thunder is walking
over the hills north of here
bringing us the rain

BAMBOO FLUTE

That's what I hear. Its high, reedy tones are as familiar and hauntingly moving as an ancestral voice, a counterpoint to the thunder rumbling farther up in the Adirondack foothills this July evening. Inviting me on a journey, more journeys than one.

I'm listening to a three-disc set I've just pulled off the shelf—archival songs from my favorite music venue. Entitled *Live at Caffe Lena* it's music recorded on the biggest little stage in the history of folk music in Saratoga Springs, New York. It ranges from folksinger Hedy West's wonderfully sardonic "Shady Grove" in 1968 up to singer-songwriter Mary Gauthier's unforgettable "I Drink" in 2013.

And now I'm shaking my head in recognition and remembrance. Recognition of the artistry and the range in that boxed set, remembrance of performances where—yup—I was in the audience. The ship of memory pulling into the pier and me hopping on board.

Which brings me to that flute. Being played by composer David Amram in his jazzy rendition of "Little Mama" back in 1974. Forgive me for name-dropping, but I am pretty sure I know that flute. Who made it. And who gave it to David.

Drop back into another July in the sixties. July of 1967 to be exact. I'm on a Benz bus with the name *God Decides* painted on its side. I'm on my way from the lorry park in

Accra, Ghana, to the University of Ghana, the Legon campus, several miles out of the city. I get off at the entrance, watch the bus disappear with its load of market women, fishermen, students, farmers, some men with colorful printed traditional cloths draped around them like togas, other men wearing the "Congo Suits" that were popularized by Kwame Nkrumah when he was president of this first black democracy in Africa. Matter of fact, I have a Congo Suit on myself, neatly cut to fit my body, short-sleeved small-collared coat, tapered slacks. It cost all of ten cedis—the equivalent of five dollars—for my local tailor in Keta to make it for me.

As I start the half-mile walk to the building that is my destination I think about the man I'm going to meet. Ephraim Amu, a distinguished professor of traditional music. I'd written him and he'd extended an invitation to come today. But as I look at my watch I wonder. It reads ten minutes before ten. Dr. Amu expects me at ten a.m.—before the midday when most people nap here in the tropics. At this rate, I'll be arriving exactly at ten. And being on time in Ghana, "uptight white people time," usually means you've gotten there too soon. For that matter, will he even be there? Why would he bother to make time for me? Me, just another *obruni*, another "white man," even if in my own mind I don't think of myself that way.

But when I knock on the door of his office a quiet, mellow voice answers "Yooo," and I find him waiting for me. A small, elderly man with a straight back, a face calm and composed, his hair slightly graying, his voice marked by the British accent of most of the men of his generation whose teachers were from the UK. Something about him seems as familiar as a grandfather. Maybe he feels my warmth toward him. When he takes my hand, his grasp is firm. He smiles and says, "Ah-ah, so you know how to do this!" when we end that shake with a snap of our middle fingers into our palms in the Ghanaian way.

Then we sit and talk about music, about the way he has taken traditional bamboo flutes and adapted them for orchestral use by making them with western tuning. About the beauty and range of the old music of his nation. It's a conversation that I believe we're both enjoying. A conversation where I listen much more than I speak.

And I leave with the gift of four of those flutes. They'll be with me for the rest of my three-year stay in Ghana as a volunteer teacher. When our secondary school gets electric guitars and a drum set and we form a school dance band, I'm ordered by Mr. Matanawui, the headmaster, to organize it. The Afro-Echoes is what the student musicians decide to name it. I'm invited to play one of my bamboo flutes with it when we do the African music called Hi-Life. And, when we do the popular Western songs our Ghanaian audiences want to hear, such as those by the Beatles and the Doors, to be the lead singer. More because I know all the words than for any vocal ability on my part.

As our gigs stretch out beyond the school to the nearby town of Keta and then throughout the Volta Region, I somehow end up with the nickname of "Jim Morrison." (Well, our lead guitar player was Kofi "Ricky Nelson" Akuaku and our bass player was Kwadzo "Elvis" Kwartey.) We're making money for the school, but I finally tell my headmaster that I appreciate his excusing me from my classes, but I really need to get back to preparing my students for their O-Level exams.

Now set the Way-Back Machine for 1970. I've returned to the United States, teaching at Skidmore College and still suffering from culture shock. Try living in a developing nation for three years where you see babies with distended bellies from malnutrition and then find yourself in the States watching a woman buy an ice-cream cone and then feed it to her poodle.

It's 1970 and all that that means. Vietnam still a bleeding wound in our nation's side. The dreams of peace and love and sharing in the sixties gradually drifting away like ships slipped loose from their moorings and being carried toward the rapids of harder drugs, conservative backlash, and trickle-down economics.

So where did I go for moments of respite? Nowhere else but the Caffe, Lena Spencer's little oasis of sanity and song. I've become one of the regulars, those Lena recognized as artists. Poets, musicians, actors. Never asked to pay the modest admission fee, I sit in the back with such close friends as folksinger Bruce "Utah" Phillips and our candle-making poet buddy Hal Noakes. Right next to Lena as she engages in endless games of Scrabble with old Tom, the former railroad man who was one of her best friends and came to the Caffe every night. This night, David Amram is performing. We end up in a long, long conversation downstairs in the Executive Bar and Grill where every performer goes after the performance. We have a mutual interest in what is now called "world music." Then I get an idea.

"Wait here," I say. "I'll be back."

I drive the six miles home and return with one of my four Ghanaian flutes.

I hand it to David without saying anything and he nods his appreciation. "I'll be playing this next weekend," he says.

I only have one of those flutes now. A year later when I saw David again, he shook his head.

"Joe," he said, I'm so sorry. That flute you gave me. I loved it, but it got broken."

So I gave him a second one. The one heard on the Caffe Lena disc.

But why do I have only one of those bamboo flutes now? Shouldn't I have two?

Well, who else in my life was a flute player? My Pueblo/ Apache friend and teacher Swift Eagle. I gave the third flute to him. It was just before he was making a trip home to Santo Domingo Pueblo.

"Joe, my friend, my friend," Swifty said, "This is soooo perfect."

I didn't quite understand what he meant by that. But I found out when he got back a few weeks later.

"The flute you gave me," he said. "When I got back to Santo Domingo I took it to our Flute Clan. And they adopted it."

A bamboo flute. I listen as it forges another link of memory and music between continents and cultures and decades.

How sweet its song.

Golden banded wings
of the monarch butterflies
unfold on milkweed

SIX DEGREES

Maybe you know that game. Six Degrees of Kevin Bacon. Where you see how many people-links it takes to get from Kevin Bacon to whichever movie star. Since he has pretty much worked with everyone in Hollywood, it's usually pretty quick. Whether living or dead or Tom Cruz or Meryl Streep.

We can all play that game, seeing how many links it takes to connect us to whoever.

One degree of me. That's how it has seemed from time to time to yours truly.

Not that I have had any contact with media and movie stars. Well, there was that time in Miami when Oprah and I were on a panel together. Or that nice letter Robert Redford sent about one of my early novels. Or the chat I had with Iroquois movie star Gary Farmer when we were both performing at the Ganondagan summer festival.

Mind you, I am not talking about Facebooking. Where we may, indeed, find ourselves hitching our wagons electronically to the elite. Maybe even earning an occasional "like," a heart-stirring "share."

No, I am referring to old-fashioned face-to-face—"I'm talking to you!"—encounters of the tangible, touchable sort.

Take that one Sunday afternoon exactly five years ago in late July when, jet-lagged and semisentient after a four a.m. departure from Oklahoma, still living on Tulsa time, I'd just stumbled up the ornate steel staircase of the then recently opened Northshire Bookstore in Saratoga Springs.

Northshire. It's a place to like in person, folks. Forget Disney World. If you're a bibliophile or biblioholic like me, you'll always find something to soothe your soul at that lovely little offspring of the original Northshire store in Manchester, Vermont.

The reason I was there was a simple one. To buy a copy of a book about the history of Caffe Lena. Apart from being America's longest running coffeehouse and a venue on whose little stage a who's who of American musicians performed, it holds a special place in my heart. Its founder, Lena Spencer, was a friend of mine. And I've been going there regularly for (counting on my martial arts–mangled fingers) nigh onto forty-five years, young feller.

The book (spoiler alert, cloyingly sweet compliment ahead) is as lovely and intelligent as Jocelyn Arem. Editor in collaboration with Caffe Lena of *Caffe Lena: Inside America's Legendary Folk Music Coffeehouse*. Jocelyn, a former Skidmore student and musician who fell in love with the Caffe and performed on that fabled stage, spent over a decade laboring mightily to bring the book together.

The ensuing slideshow and armchair discussion between Jocelyn and Sarah Craig, the Caffe's prestidigitacious manager was warm, relaxed, and inspiring. Like a night at Lena's. It made me want to leap up and purchase copies for all my close friends. Both of them.

But the coincidence that prompted this navel-gazing self-aggrandizing post occurred before Sarah and Jocelyn began to speak. Two young folk musicians who'd be performing at Lena's that evening were introduced. Nora Jane Struthers and her partner P. J. George. Dang, they were good. Only two songs, but their musicality, their spot-on harmonies, and Nora Jane's just plain fine lyrics won everyone over.

But for some reason, though I was pretty sure I'd never seen them before, their performance inspired one of those

Yogi Berra moments for me. No, not the one when the fabled former big league catcher, manager, and master of fractured logic stated, "We wouldn't have lost if you hadn't beaten us." Nor, "Nobody goes there anymore. It's too crowded."

I am referring to his famous quip: "It's déjà vu all over again."

Naturally I went to the Caffe that night to see Nora Jane Struthers and her band, the Party Line. There my buddy and ace bassist Ed Lowman was already seated at a table and beckoned for me to join him.

No big deal about that coincidence. Nothing like the time I was in the Chicago airport and saw a man who looked familiar—though shorn of his usual prophetic beard. And with a cast on his leg.

"Allen?" I said.

"Joe?" he replied.

Yup. None other than Allen Ginsberg, who I knew from several other past meetings.

Historical footnote: *why* Allen Ginsberg, world famous poet of the Beat Generation, might remember *moi*.

Perhaps because of our first meeting after he gave a reading at Syracuse University. I was a grad student then. Rolled up to the house where the after-party was happening. Well, actually roared up. I rode a Harley then. A 1950s 1130 cc beast with a suicide shift on the tank. In retrospect, I was a fairly impressive sight. Leathers, boots, full-face beard. (See gifted musicians we've ever known. He's also one of those people that crazy things happen to.

A year or so ago Tom showed up at the annual gathering at Norridgewock, Maine, where Wabanaki people gather to remember the events that took place there. August 22, 1724. The English came and encircled the village where Father Sebastian Rasles had established his Catholic church and was a dear friend to the Wabanakiak. Few Native men were there that day to defend the village. Eighty or more, mostly women and children and old people, died when the English and their Mohawk mercenaries opened fire.

At that gathering Tom showed up in a relatively new Volvo, a better car than he'd had before.

"A moose got this for me," he said.

He'd been driving down pretty much the same stretch of road we were on. Next thing he knew a moose had come through the windshield and was in his lap. Tom was unhurt, though neither moose nor car survived. He got both his moose that year and his new car.

We were two hours into our drive. We'd just stopped in Farmington for dinner. Discovered a restaurant we'd never been to before. And, despite the fact that Columbus Day was almost upon us, we'd refrained from taking ownership of it by Right of Discovery.

"Columbus Day," the African American comedian and civil rights activist Dick Gregory said to me back in 1970 when he came to speak at Skidmore College, and we renewed an acquaintance that began when we first met on the Meredith March in Mississippi in the summer of 1966. "Why would anybody celebrate a day honoring a man who come and laid claim to someplace other folk already owned? Next Columbus Day, why don't you and me walk downtown and discover us a new Cadillac?"

Getting back to that restaurant, its name was Thai Smile. The menu was terrific and the food we got was incredible. Fresh, perfectly spiced, served with style. It had to be the best Thai food we'd ever eaten in New England north of Boston. Check the place out next time you are in Farmington, Maine.

So there we were, cruising along. Jesse driving. Both of us feeling a bit blissed out after that meal and the two days spent with such great folks as Roger Paul—a Passamaquoddy/Maliseet Language keeper and educator who is a gifted storyteller, ranking with the best tellers I've ever seen. Remember that name. Roger Paul. He deserves a national audience beyond the many admiring Native and non-Native fans he already has in Maine.

His delivery and his physical presence are amazing. We loved the way Roger stumbled about like a zombie as he explained how the Great Mystery told the animals to be really careful with those new beings coming to earth. Those human beings. Those dopey, clumsy ones who were going to be afraid of everything. Especially each other.

"Be real careful not to scare them," the animals were told.

As we drove through the deepening dark, Jess and I were talking about the usual things. The story Tom told about getting his moose car, the multiple meanings of the Native place names we passed, the differences between Western Abenaki and Passamaquoddy, the importance of being able to invert during my rolls as a seventy-five year-old black belt. Typical father-and-son stuff.

We were also making the kind of silly remarks to each other that used to make my wife, Carol, say, "Joseph, stop it. Now!"

Such as, "Think the border between New Hampshire and Maine will be open?" And, "Are we going to have to pay duty on these potatoes we're importing?" Or, "Oh, no! That sign said no out-of-state firewood. What are we going to do with this box of matches?" Or, looking at the dotted line drawn across the map on our GPS marking the border, "Make sure we steer in between those lines when we enter the state! Don't want a collision!"

Then I saw the first of those signs that appear at the New Hampshire border. I read it out loud in a normal conversational tone. "Brake for Moose."

At exactly the same time as a large white moth came winging out of the dark woods toward the driver's side of our Altima.

"MOOSE!" Jesse yelled as he braked and turned the wheel to avoid what his peripheral vision had magnified. And we slid sideways into New Hampshire.

With the spirits of the *moosak* laughing at us humans who are so easily scared.

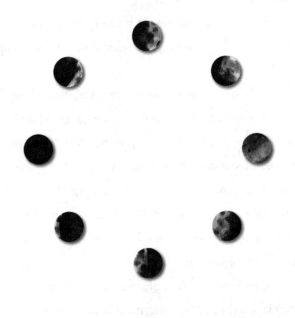

MZATONOS

MOON OF FREEZING

THIN ICE

I wake up with the pond on my mind.

When I look out the window, I see that the once-deep tracks of the deer across the yard have collapsed into shadowed furrows.

Boots on. Coat, gloves, snowshoes taken down from the wall.

Bear paws is what they are called for their shape, an old Abenaki design. And these particular snowshoes are old ones. Sinew stretched over a bent ash frame, not some space-age stuff strung across aluminum. Once my father's they're more than twice my age. Made by one of the Sabattis family,

197

a descendent of Mitchell Sabattis, the famous Adirondack guide who lived at Long Lake, eighty miles to the north of here.

Ogemakw is our name for snowshoes. And *ogema* the name for the white ash tree from which they're made. In so many cases, if you know the name for something you also know what gift it may give you. Just as the birch is *mask-wamozi*, the blanket tree.

Live 10,000 years in the same environment and you, too, may find that your language reflects the gifts that everything around you may offer. If you're paying attention and listening.

I step outside and the clear air cleanses my lungs. The powdery snow that was eighteen inches deep four mornings ago is now just a flattened crust that crunches under my weight as I walk. Here and there earth is visible. Brown grass, the strew of needles from the tall pines, twigs, and bare soil.

I take the trail that leads down to Bucket Pond. At first, I see no new sign other than my own tracks. But just because it's unseen doesn't mean that a whole weave of life is not present in these winter woods. That's why I walk slow, stop now and then. Move too fast and you miss it. Like that hole in the snow near the base of a beech sapling. A little scatter of dirt in front of it marks the quick emergence and scuttle across the snow to a second hole across from it. Just big enough to fit my little finger.

Much too small for a chipmunk—or a red squirrel like the one who perches defiantly on my feeder each morning. One white-circled eye cocked toward my window over the sink, it hunches its back against the complaints of the chickadees its arrival always evicts.

That tunnel in the snow could only be that of a shrew. The fierce little furnace of its breath needs more refueling for its size than almost any other animal. If I ate like a shrew, I'd be consuming a pickup load of grub each day.

On farther down the hill and I'm at the edge. Bucket Pond. So called not for its shape or any resemblance to a pail, but after the Bucket Family that once held the deed. And Lavender's Pond for a time before that. More than a century ago—or so my grandfather told me.

"One of them Lavenders drowned herself here. And there was reports of some seeing her ghost."

I've not seen or felt her presence. But this ridge has ghosts aplenty. Some far older than that woman of the Lavender family whose first name I'll likely never know.

Here in these hills my family and I have done what we can to protect burial places that were here long before our newer relatives from across the ocean began to put their names on Ndakinna, our old land.

I stand by the pond for a time. Just looking. Just listening. No wind blowing, so the soughing voices of the pines are silent. But there are more stories to be read in the ice that's begun to thicken again now that the temperature dropped well below freezing for two days and nights in a row.

The light snow on top of the ice has turned the pond into a sort of journal, keeping record of everything that has passed. My own tracks intersect and cross those of the flock of turkeys that come each day to pick up corn that we leave out by the pines, tracks of rabbits, of squirrels. And over here the distinctive paw prints—three at a time—of a fisher following the trail of a rabbit.

The arcing lines of deer tracks are the most visible. Four deer at least crossed here when the snow and ice on the pond were little more than slush. Deep tracks. Each hoof drag, usually just a thin line between one print and the next, is a deep furrow.

When I reach the pond, just as I expected, the ice now seems thick enough for me to walk across. Plus, on snowshoes, my weight will be more widely distributed, less likely to break through. Just in case, though, I've brought with me a pole made from one of the small maples I trimmed out of the grapevines this past summer. I hold it with both hands across my chest as I take my first steps out onto the ice.

It's a trick I learned back in 1992 when I was on Baffin Island, recording old stories from such Inuit elders as Luccasie Nuturaluk. The sea ice there is rubbery from the salt in it, pushed up at times by the action of wave and wind into pressure ridges as high as ten feet tall. A hunter can spot a seal from the top of such ridges. However, because it is always in motion, because the depth and strength of that ice can vary, one wrong step and you'll break through. But if you hold your long harpoon—or a pole—across your body you won't go any farther than your chest. And you can use that pole or harpoon to help pull yourself out.

The name of a poet friend comes to me as I remember that. How many winters ago was it when Hugh lost his life when the ice gave way as he was crossing one of those Maine lakes he loved to write about? What a fragile line there is between this life and whatever follows it. How little it takes for us to pass from this world.

Just one wrong step.

I walk out a few yards, then listen. A winter pond answers you at times as your weight presses down. A low moan as ice presses onto unfrozen water. Then a crackling sound— like a giant piece of cellophane—as a hidden wave bounces back from the far shore and displaced ice begins to break. But I don't hear anything yet.

Unlike that day when I was on the frozen skin of Lake Champlain, that huge, long lake my Abenaki ancestors called Petonbowk, the Waters Between. I was staying in a cabin on the western shore along the upper part of the lake where it is divided by islands. And when I woke on a cold sunny morning, the first things that caught my eye were the bear paw snowshoes propped in the corner. It was early enough that I could make it to Valcour Island and back before I had to do the lecture and class visits my hosts at Plattsburgh State had set up for me.

There'd been a thaw the week before, but the ice was still thick. Or so I was told. At least three feet. People had been on the ice fishing the day before, driving snowmobiles back and forth. I'd even seen someone a mile or so out driving a car with chains on its tires.

I'd been walking for half an hour when I heard it. A distant THWUM! Like a gut-deep note plucked on the lowest strings of the world's biggest bass fiddle.

Then another noise, a loud CRACK!

Followed by a far-off sighing sound—like a giant letting out a long, long breath.

I looked toward the far shore and saw something. A dark line being drawn by an invisible pencil. A line that was being made by the surface ice opening a long crevice.

It was heading directly my way. No point in running. Or in being afraid as that break in the ice flowed toward me like a slow-motion bolt of frozen lightning.

I just remember thinking, "This is really interesting!"

It shot straight at me, then passed between my feet, spreading them out, out, into a half split and then—before I lost my balance and fell into the water I could see below me— that crevice closed up, and I was standing there as if nothing had happened.

But something had. I did not continue on to Valcour Island that morning. I headed back to the cabin, pausing only to say, "*Wliwini,*" and place a handful of tobacco on the ice of the old lake that had decided not to swallow me that morning.

The ice of Bucket Pond today is translucent. Not white, almost purple. Nor is it smooth. It's dappled with little bumps, almost as if it caught the wind as it reformed from sludge into a solid. It's not skating ice—unless you enjoy jarring your bones and hearing your teeth rattle.

In the middle of the pond, three of those deer trails I've been following suddenly loop off to either side. They almost make a double-curve design like the uncurling fern shapes etched into the birch bark of our old lodges. The fourth deer trail in the middle suddenly widens at its center. But it doesn't end there, it continues on.

When I get closer I can see what happened. That wide space at the center, almost a circle of ice that looks darker because you can see through it to the water beneath, that is where the deer fell through. The trail that continues shows the deer pulled itself out, managed frantically, from the skewed shapes of its track, to get off the pond to the other side.

THUNK!

Oops.

I know what that voice is telling me. Rather than be the causal agent for yet another circle in the ice, I turn slowly.

Head back with careful steps. Thankful for yet another lesson. Walking slow to reach the shore.

Walking, as we all do every day that we breathe, on thin ice.

Ice in the bucket
mirroring the clouded sky
cold breeze in my face

Juniper berries
bright red on the green branches
glow above the snow

NEW SNOW

It fell last night. A half inch or so on top of the two inches that had mantled the hilltop thus far this early winter. It's what some would call a dusting—though it's whiter, cleaner than that.

It's as if the dark slate of world has been wiped clean. The fallen leaves and needles are hidden, the land as smooth and untroubled as the face of a peacefully sleeping child.

I go outside onto the deck. My bare feet sink into the snow as I walk slowly, the weight and warmth of my soles melting tracks. The exact shapes of my feet are there from heels to toes. My feet. Recognizable from anyone else's by their imperfections. By, for example, the way the once-broken little toe on my left foot presses in against its neighbor.

I take one long step into the middle of the deck. Exhale. Bend my knees, feel the top of my head connected to the clouds. Raise my arms to the sky, then let them slowly fall into Embrace Tiger, rise up toward Return to Mountain. Breathe. Breathe out for a thousand miles. Turn. The Tree on the Hilltop that Sees in All Directions.

Time goes somewhere else. So do I.

One more deep exhalation and I complete the form that I began to learn from Chungliang Al Huang more than twenty winters ago.

Perhaps I have not done it correctly. Well, no "perhaps" about it. Nowhere near as good as a tai chi master or even a dedicated student. Sloppy, in fact.

I smile at the thought of how a teacher might have corrected my stance, my steps, the speed of my motions, the positions of my hands.

So imperfect.

So what?

What is perfection if not vanity?

And what I've done was not for a teacher, a class, a competition. Or even for myself.

It was just . . . done.

I jump backward a few feet. The pattern of that ancient form is there marked in the snow, the precise prints of my feet like brush strokes on parchment. If the sun shines just enough today, each footprint will become glazed with blue ice—like the prints I left four days ago in the first winter snow that fell, prints erased by this latest snowfall.

The one constant in our lives is change. In the end nothing solid will remain. But the flow of spirit will always continue. That's a concept that may be easier to explain in the Abenaki language—in which everything is verb-based—than in overly literal English. Or perhaps it is better not explained but instead embodied by the movement of a body through space. Illustrated by footprints left on the transient page of an early December snow.

I stand there, that silly smile still on my face. The mercury in the thermometer next to me is below the freezing line. I'm out here in my undershorts and without a shirt. Craaazzy. Good thing our camp is at the end of a long driveway out of sight of other houses and the town road. Who needs to see a seminaked septuagenarian seemingly freezing his butt off at this time of the morning? Probably time to go back in before my wife, Nicola, comes out to remind me that she cares enough about me to not want me to suffer hypothermia.

But I feel surrounded by warmth. And I'm remembering what my first martial arts teacher told me.

"When you feel cold, open your coat."
New snow.

Changing wind blows cold
sun reflecting off new snow
white covers brown leaves

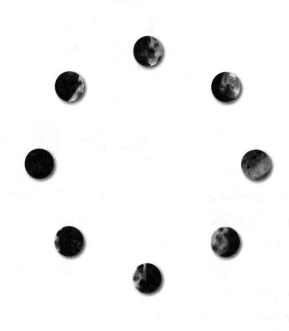

PEBONKAS

MOON OF LONG NIGHTS

FIRE MAKING

That's something I've always been good at. And during this time of year, the Moon of Long Nights, here in the Adirondack Mountain foothills, making fire is on my mind every day.

I crouch down in front of the woodstove, almost in the posture of someone about to prostrate himself in prayer. Then I touch a single match to the crumpled handful of paper beneath the carefully stacked dry twigs and small branches that I gathered from the woods that come within a hundred feet of my back door.

On top of those small branches are crisscrossed split pieces of cherry, maple, birch, ash, or oak. Hardwood cut several seasons ago and dried till the ends of each piece are cracked—checked, a sign of seasoning. No pine or spruce or hemlock, softwoods fine for burning outdoors, but far too pitchy, too full of resinous sap to use inside—unless you are a fan of chimney fires. The sooty buildup may be so thick and black that a stovepipe will turn red hot and begin to shoot little bombs of burning creosote—KA-POOF! KA-POOF! KA-POOF!—up into the sky, even after the fire in the stove below it has been put out.

I remember one memorable night having to climb a ladder up onto my sister Mary Ann's house next door to ours, thick gloves on my hands, to yank off one of those cannoning stovepipes and toss it down into the deep snow—where it immediately melted its way out of sight like a diving submarine.

Fire, one of our oldest and most desired friends. It seems as if every culture has their own story of how fire came to the people. Just as the Greeks tell of Prometheus stealing it from the gods, our Algonquin traditions here in the Northeast talk of the time when humans had no fire and it had to be stolen by a boy from selfish monsters who killed all those who ventured too close to their domain. Fox, who aided that boy by carrying a burning stick in its mouth, still has black lips as a result.

And just as it is useful, so, too, fire is dangerous. In another of our ancient tales, our culture hero Gluskonba engages in conversation with Ktsi Nwaskw, the Great

Mystery who created all things, about how things should be in the world.

"Should fire burn all the time and never go out?" Ktsi Nwaskw asks.

"*Nda*," Gluskonba replies. "No. That would not do. For if a person was burned and fire could not go out, then that person would surely die. But if that fire could be put out, then the burn could get well."

As I close the door of the stove on the fire that has already begun to whisper its ancient song, I think about my grandparents' house where I was raised. Seven miles down the mountain from this cabin, away from the distractions of televisions or phone calls, the house on the corner of Middle Grove Road and Route 9N is still the place I call home. My grandfather built it on top of the stone foundation of the house that had belonged to my great-grandparents, Ed and Flora Dunham.

That original house was burned to the ground nearly a hundred years ago. On purpose. The fire was set by a man named Hayes who held a grudge against Ed Dunham. Hayes was a bootlegger and a dangerous man. Ed had sold him a load of cider that had gone hard and then—at the urging of my great-grandma, a staunch member of the Women's Christian Temperance Union—told the sheriff about the sale, since he knew that cider would be used to make liquor.

When Hayes found out who had told the sheriff he began to take his revenge. Their collie dogs were poisoned by strychnine hidden in pieces of meat tossed to them. Their cider mill across the street was burned down. So was their sawmill on Dunham Brook three miles away. Their cows were shot in the fields, their favorite horse, Starbaby Lee, found in its stall with its throat cut. Finally, their house was burned and they barely escaped alive.

Hayes was a thorough fellow when it came to revenge. An eye for an eye was just a starting point.

And, as I've explained at greater length in my autobiography, *Bowman's Store*, no one was every prosecuted for those crimes. People, even lawmen, were too afraid of Hayes, who worked as a railroad detective, carried two pearl-handled revolvers, and was brazen enough to hijack loads of liquor being brought down from Canada by the crews of such infamous criminals as Legs Diamond.

I still, every now and then when I'm working the flower beds around the back side of my grandparents' home, find twisted lumps of semitransparent green that once were vases or drinking glasses. Melted by that spiteful blaze.

With a history like that as a part of my childhood, I grew up with a healthy respect for fire. But my childhood also forged a closer relationship with fire than most—old or young—have today. Our stove in the kitchen, which both heated the house and was used for cooking, used wood.

Restocking the ever-hungry woodbox from the cords of fire-wood stacked outside was one of my everyday chores. My old friend Bill Smith from Colton, New York, the finest Adirondack storyteller living, recites a poem he wrote about the woodbox he always had to replenish as a kid. How in dreams it comes back to haunt him, saying, "Fill me up again!"

Firewood warms you at least four times. The first is when you cut it. The second when you split and stack it. The third when you lug it into the house. And the fourth is when you burn it. My two sons learned that lesson when they were little, and I'd take them with me into the woods to load the old truck with the firewood I'd cut with the chain saw.

I imagine that my older son, Jim, still has his own nightmares of being back in those woods while I kept sawing away, making more mountains of logs for them to lug.

"Dad just keeps cutting," Jim would whisper in a desperate voice to his more stoic younger brother, Jesse. "Please, God, make him stop."

Not that he didn't have his own strategy to lessen their workload. I'd only find out years later that when my back was turned Jim would be rolling a good number of those logs down into the gully off the wood road so that they wouldn't have to unload them back home.

The irony, of course, is that Jim, who founded our Ndakinna Education Center, now has his own special relationship with fire. Among other things, he teaches how to make fire the traditional way with a bow drill—a skill he's mastered so well that he can create a coal in less than ten seconds. Add to that the interesting fact that with homes, fireplaces, and woodstoves of their own, both Jim and Jesse are not averse to taking advantage of the fact that their dad is still fairly handy with a chain saw. Such as two mornings ago when Jesse came up to the camp to pick up a load of firewood from me when his stockpile ran out at exactly the same time as his propane.

Knowing how to make fire has served me well over the years. Every now and then I look up at the wall and see a photo of my younger self, when I had long hair and a mustache, sitting cross-legged on a boulder. Framed with that photo is my ticket to the Woodstock Music Festival. A ticket that was never collected because by the time I got there, our car moving slower than a snail along the roads clogged for forty miles in every direction, all the fences had been flattened, and it was being announced over the loudspeakers that it was now a free festival.

What did fire have to do with my days at White Lake? (Which, rather than the actual town called Woodstock, is where the epic event took place on Max Yasgur's farm.) Well, when the darkness came, the four friends I'd ridden with unrolled their sleeping bags next to their car to spend the night. Others were doing the same thing in the surrounding fields. Unlike Woodstock Two (where my son Jesse was one of the Native American performers who opened that even more anarchic and out-of-control rerun), a lot of people did not have tents.

But I could feel that rain was coming.

The only thing I'd brought with me was a change of underwear and a small pillow wrapped in a bedroll made of two blankets tied with a long length of nylon cord. I climbed over a stone wall and made my way into a nearby patch of woods. I used one of my blankets, tied at an angle between trees, to make a sort of lean-to. I gathered fallen branches, cleared a space next to my shelter, piled a ring of stones, and started a fire with the matches I had in my pocket. Thus when the rain began to fall, wrapped in my other blanket I slept peacefully through that night, only waking up once to add more wood to my small fire.

While my friends who had retreated into their car after the downpour, woke up cold and wet, I was dry and rested.

My novel *Killer of Enemies* imagines a future world where electricity doesn't work. And my main character, a young Chiricahua Apache woman, is an expert at the old skills of survival. Which includes, of course, making fire. Tu Books, my publishers, asked me if I could do a short video to post on their website about some of those old skills.

Can you guess what my answer was to their burning question? Yup. A five-minute piece that focused on . . . *Skweda*. Fire. Capably filmed and excellently edited by Eric Jenks (whom we took captive when he was but a child and intend to keep as long as he does our every bidding now that he's the assistant director of our Ndakinna Education Center), it shows me talking about fire making and then Jim making an actual fire with a bow drill and a tinder bundle. With flute music in the background composed and performed by Jesse.

Making fire. As I write those words again I realize that I have so many more stories I could tell about that. From my years in Ghana, from the trips my sons Jim and Jesse and I took to Mali and Mexico in 1992. From a high mountaintop in eastern Oregon. From East Germany before the fall of the Berlin Wall. From the heart of Great Meadow Correctional Facility where I taught and ran a college program for eight years. From the woods behind Ray Fadden's Six Nations Museum in Onchiota, New York.

But I suppose I've written enough for now about making fire.

Beech leaves don't let go
after frost they still hang on
flutter in the wind

Deep snow in the woods
walking is not easy now
deer leaving wide trails

BREATHE

It's late December and I'm on an airplane.

One of the people a few rows ahead was having a panic attack a few minutes ago. Not an unusual thing to have happen on a plane these days. It took two attendants to talk that person down, convince him everything was all right.

"Just breathe," I heard one of them say to him.

Good advice, I thought. *Breathe*.

Breathing. That's something we all do all the time—those of us still among the living. In and out. Breath after breath, usually without thinking about it. Unless we are winded. Finding it hard, after running or any sort of heavy exertion, to "catch our breath," as the saying goes.

As a martial arts teacher I see it all the time. People breathing hard, red faced and panting, feeling as if they can't go on.

It's almost always the same at the start of studying a martial art, when your belt is white—not yet darkened by the necessary grime of decades of training, by dirt and sweat, by blood and by tears. You struggle, your breathing as ragged as a ripped cloth, gasping like a fish flopped out onto the shore. And you think—be honest—about giving up.

And that is when you need to just breathe. Slow. Slow and controlled.

I've been saying that for four decades to my students. I should say my fellow students because I'm still learning. It's as true of the martial disciplines as it is of any artful pursuit. Good old Geoffrey Chaucer, the English poet, nailed it back in the fourteenth century when he wrote "the lyf so short, the craft so longe to lerne." Whether it is pentjak silat or tai chi or Brazilian jiujitsu or writing, the lesson is the same. Be patient. Take it slow.

Find your breath. Then you won't lose it.

Don't fight with your breath. Fight *with* your breath.

Here is a simple teaching related to that, a method you can put into practice right away.

Smell the rose.

Blow out the candle.

It's a Zen teaching. It's well known to the practitioners of that revered way toward spiritual awakening, as well as those who teach the way of the fist. It was not passed to me by any one particular teacher. Gison Tenaga, Al Huang, T. T. Lliang, Jacare Cavacante or any number of others might all take credit for teaching it to me at the start of one journey or another on the warrior's path. I've also read it in many different books—and seen it on the screen.

As a matter of fact, the most recent time I heard that old teaching was on an episode of the cable show *Ax Men*. It was spoken by a slightly panicked lumberman trying to calm himself down enough to run a cable pulling logs up a rough northwestern mountain without killing his fellow workers downslope from him. He was using, effectively it turned out, a mantra he said was taught him by a meditation teacher. It doesn't matter where you get a useful teaching—as long as you get it.

Smell the rose.

Blow out the candle.

As I watched that show I found myself wondering if that California logger's teacher had any connection to the roshi of my old friend Steve Sanfield.

Steve Sanfield, my late friend, was a devoted student of Zen. Poet and storyteller, chronicler of the fools of Chelm and the heroes of Black history, he could be grouchy and generous in the same breath. He was as white-bearded and venerable in his last years as Walt Whitman—though much less self-absorbed.

As I write Steve's name I find myself standing again with him one last summer, in front of the North San Juan school-house in the California mountains, posing for a photo. Bill Harley, our musician-storyteller buddy, has his arms around us both. We're at the Sierra Storytelling festival Steve helped found. I'm hearing the amused, slightly self-deprecating tone in his voice as he answers us when we ask when he's going to be back up on stage himself.

"No," he says, "I think those days are gone now."

Then the two of us walk together. Steve's steps are slow as walking meditation, one slow foot after another as if measuring the breath he had left, measuring it no longer in years but in weeks. But he was still smiling as he breathed. Out and in.

In and out, out and in and then—in one last exhalation—blowing out the last candle, returning his breath to the winds of the Sierra Nevada, misting into the autumn rain, joining the center of the first flakes of winter snow, absorbed as a gift by the thirsty land, part of a cycle that never ends. Breathing out as others breathe out and in.

Breathing in. Inspiration. We breathe it all in, all that was shared before us. The beauty, the pain, the uncertainty, and the immense, never-ending flow all around us. Inspiring every word, every thought, every breath that we return to the life we do not own but only borrow with our lungs.

Think of where we are. At the bottom of the greatest of all oceans, the sea of air that we seldom see or even consider as it embraces us. This planet's atmosphere is—as my Native elders so often have reminded me—along with sunlight and water, one of the three life-giving gifts we neither purchase nor own. Great gifts we seldom remember to acknowledge.

So, as I write this in my notebook, encased by the steel skin of US Airways 321, I listen to the sound of the jet engines, revving louder as they gulp in that air. I hear the whirr of the air conditioner pumping in enough of that life-giving atmosphere to sustain our bodies through the long flight from one coast to another. I breathe in and out again.

Smell the rose.

Blow out the candle.

And I whisper these words, shared now with you at the end of this year, at the end of this brief journey through a year of moons.

Let us give thanks for this blessing.
give thanks for this gift
of breath, of breath
so freely granted
that we may live.

Let us give thanks
as we travel together,
give thanks,
give thanks
that we
breathe.

Dusty snow blowing
across the trail as we walk
covering our prints

ABOUT
THE AUTHOR

Joseph Bruchac lives in the Adirondack Mountain foothills town of Greenfield Center, New York, in the same house where his maternal grandparents raised him. Much of his writing draws on that land and his Native American ancestry. Although his northeastern American Indian heritage is only one part of an ethnic background that includes Slovak and English blood, those Native roots are the ones by which he has been most nourished.